A GUIDE TO THE

Mermaid
Tarot

About the Author

Leeza Robertson spends more time with tarot cards than she does real people. You will find her hidden away in warm, cozy corners with piles of decks and books around her. She spends her days dreaming up new decks and exploring ways to introduce more people to the world of tarot. When she doesn't have her nose inside a book or her fingers dancing across a deck of cards, she is hiking, traveling, and finding new books to stick her nose into. Connect with Leeza on Twitter: @Leeza_Robertson.

About the Artist

Julie Dillon (Los Angeles, CA) is a freelance artist whose clients include Simon & Schuster, Penguin, Tor, and Wizards of the Coast. She is the winner of several Hugo, Chesley, and Locus awards for best artist.

A GUIDE TO THE
Mermaid
Tarot

Leeza Robertson

ILLUSTRATED BY
Julie Dillon

LLEWELLYN PUBLICATIONS — WOODBURY, MINNESOTA

FIRST EDITION
Fourth Printing, 2020

Book design: Cassie Willett
Cover design: Shira Atakpu
Cover and interior card art: Julie Dillon
Editing: Laura Kurtz

Llewellyn Publications is a registered trademark of Llewellyn Worldwide Ltd.

Library of Congress Cataloging-in-Publication Data
ISBN: 978-0-7387-5109-2
The Mermaid Tarot consists of a boxed set of 78 color cards and this book.

Llewellyn Worldwide Ltd. does not participate in, endorse, or have any authority or responsibility concerning private business transactions between our authors and the public.

All mail addressed to the author is forwarded, but the publisher cannot, unless specifically instructed by the author, give out an address or phone number.

Any Internet references contained in this work are current at publication time, but the publisher cannot guarantee that a specific location will continue to be maintained. Please refer to the publisher's website for links to authors' websites and other sources.

Llewellyn Publications
A Division of Llewellyn Worldwide Ltd.
2143 Wooddale Drive
Woodbury, MN 55125-2989
www.llewellyn.com

Printed in China

Contents

1   **An Introductory Note**

5   **Chapter 1**
The Flow of the Deck

11   **Chapter 2**
Taking the Cards for a Swim

19   **Chapter 3**
The Major Arcana

87   **Chapter 4**
The Minor Arcana

      Cups 89

      Wands.................... 133

      Pentacles 177

      Swords 217

261   **Chapter 5**
Mermaids Magic and Spreads

273   **A Final Note**

An
Introductory Note

This deck has a very interesting creation story, one that has woven itself into each of the cards that you now hold in your hands. It all started with a single irritating idea … an idea that just would not go away and die somewhere quietly. Instead, it kept showing up in my life in the most annoying ways. Everywhere I turned was a picture, song, book, CD, or conversation around the theme of this deck. No matter how hard I tried, I just could not get away from this idea. After reading *Big Magic* by Elizabeth Gilbert I thought perhaps I could transfer this idea to someone else, much how Gilbert herself wrote about transferring ideas via a kiss. However, it only lead to me being contracted to produce this deck, so thanks for nothing, *Big Magic*!

I am going to be totally honest here: mermaids were never really my thing. We all tend to gravitate to specific areas of interest that for whatever reason become the things we love. Mermaids never really held that sort of interest to me, or at least not consciously. But having now completed this deck, I see how they have always been here—they have always lurked in the water of my subconscious mind, waiting for the right set of conditions to make their way to the surface. I see now that all this time, they have been guiding me, protecting me, and even partly influencing bits and pieces of my experience without me even knowing. It all ties in to my love of the sea.

I have always had a special bond to the sea, one that wasn't fully realized until I left my landlocked home in the Australian bush and moved to the bay side city of Melbourne. Here I discovered many new worlds, and the one that had the most impact on my life was the ocean itself. I moved to a suburb that was right on the water, where the beach and the call of the waves rang through the wind every morning.

My days and nights revolved around how many more hours it would be until I could jump into the waves and swim as far as my legs could carry me. Swimming under a full moon was always one of my joys, especially if there was no wind and the bay was as still as a millpond. Those nights seemed magical and surreal and allowed me to live in a world totally separate from the life I was living on land. The ocean waves and the siren song of the sea were always tempting me, begging me to be by their side.

As life moved on, I moved to a suburb that was not as close to the water and started a family. Like me, my children all heard the call of the sea's song, and we spent many days and nights at the beach jumping in waves, building sand castles, and letting the ocean fill us with magic and wonder that we so missed once we were away from its shore line.

Life moved on, children grew, lives changed, and people moved. Now I live in the desert, far from the oceans edge, but I still hear its song and its call. After all, it is the same ocean— the same expanse of water that has been with me since the beginning. I guess that is why I consider the Pacific Ocean *my* ocean, for even here in the desert, it is never too far away. When it calls, I always come.

Many a friend has pointed out how much I have been in denial about my link to mermaid and mer-folk energy, but I truly never saw a connection, or at least not until this project demanded to be created and birthed into the world. Creating this deck has taught me about timing, flow, and how when something is ready to burst forth in your life, it will. The mermaids have obviously been with me my whole life; I didn't need to acknowledge them for it to be true, nor did I even have to like them for them to stick around. In fact, I didn't even really believe in them, but here they are anyway. I have never been known as a mermaid person, but you now hold in your hands proof to the contrary. Sometimes we don't even know what we don't know until we know it.

Tarot decks take a village to create. It is not just the deck creator and the artist. There is a whole team of people who lovingly shape and birth these projects into the world. I have been blessed to have the most amazing creative team at Llewellyn, and bringing artist Julie Dillon on board for this deck was just the icing on the cake. I knew the moment I saw Julie's very first sketch that we had something special. I may have created the world for these mermaids to re-tell the tarot's story, but Julie has brought that story to life…and now you get to hold it in your hands.

Seeing how an artist interprets my written world-building is awe inspiring. Each artist brings something different to a deck, and you never know how the energy is going to come together until the first couple of cards are under our belt. With the guidance of our team's art director and project manager, we have pulled our collective talents together to create something we feel is both intimately entwined with mermaid mythology and different enough so you feel like you are entering a whole new world, where you can experience a new creation story of your own. It's a watery world where lessons, blessings, and challenges will guide you onto a new path or possibly even a new adventure.

From every person who helped bring this beautiful tarot deck into the world, we hope you enjoy your time swimming in the magical world of the mermaids.

Chapter 1

THE FLOW OF THE DECK

One of the things that makes tarot *tarot* is that it has structure, order, and flow to its three acts. These three acts or parts are in every tarot deck, and they allow you to explore spiritual processes, stages of development, and lessons in everyday tasks. It is this specific system and structure that differentiates a tarot deck from a normal oracle deck. If you have a deck that does not have seventy-eight cards broken up into the three acts of the majors, courts, and minors, you do not have a tarot deck in your hands.

Each tarot deck interprets the concepts and ideas of the seventy-eight cards in a unique way. Here in the Mermaid Tarot, you will notice the story, ideas, and concepts of the cards have been told through the lens of mermaid mythology. Each part of this deck adds to the many stories already written about those who live under the water, deep beneath the surface.

MAJOR ARCANA

The twenty-two cards of the major arcana have been created to not only take you on a journey from one cycle to the next but also offer a spiritual and philosophical lesson in each card. In many respects, we are all the Fool, birthed from the waves and sea foam, learning how to navigate the many obstacles the land of humans poses. The journey of the fool, you and me, its lesson and challenges are mapped out through the cards of the major arcana numbered 0 through 21, the Magician to the World. Think of the mer-folk of the major arcana as your teachers and guides. Listen to the wisdom they impart, and see how they show you how to navigate the land, air, fire, and water of the tarot empire.

THE MINOR ARCANA AND COURT CARDS

To understand the different stages you will go through as you make your way around the tarot empire, a full cast of royal courts are waiting to assist you. The kings and queens of the Mermaid Tarot are gods and goddesses in their own right—they have power, prestige, and thousands of years of knowledge to share with you. They will each demonstrate different ways to lead, inspire, protect, and govern. They will show you how to not only create but be a good steward of your creations. They will also instruct you on how to provide a safe space for your creations to grow and expand. Pay attention as they show you how a community under good leadership can serve and benefit all.

The knights of the Mermaid Tarot share lessons in honor, respect, and duty. They remind us of all the things that can and should be done for the betterment of our lives and the community we live in. The knights can often carry messages from one kingdom to the next, but it will be up to you to hear and receive the messages they bring. Most times, these messages are about the less exciting aspects of life, so it is not uncommon to pretend not to hear them. The knights prepare us for larger roles in our community and remind us to sharpen our skills and stick to good, productive habits.

The pages connect us to the energy and wonder of the inner child, back to the time when we were just learning about who we are and discovering who we might like to be when we grow up. The pages encourage curiosity and offer us a space to play with the elements and ideas of each of the tarot kingdoms. In many ways, the pages are a first step or introduction to a concept, idea, process, approach, or skill. It is with the pages we learn new habits that we go forth to strengthen and master when we become knights.

Each of the court cards represents a step or stage along the path of the Fool's Journey. Beginning a new skill or habit under the pages, we train it and refine it, taking the next leap into the knights until eventually all of that practice, commitment, and determination pay off as we advance to the queens and kings. It is under the queens and kings that the spark of the page steps into its true power.

THE MINOR ARCANA: THE SUITS ACE TO TEN

The cards marked ace through to ten are the last cards of the minor arcana. These cards show the four mermaid kingdoms going about their daily tasks. The kingdom of wands is represented by the guardians of the volcanoes here. The kingdom of pentacles is represented in this deck by the guardians of lakes, rivers, and waterfalls. These mer-folk look after all land-based waterways. The kingdom of cups is represented by the guardians of the deep ocean. They reside in the never-ending vast spaces of the sea and control the wild currents, manage the weather, and patrol the deepest darkest caverns. The kingdom of swords is filled with the guardians of the polar ice caps. Harsh terrain, isolation, and wilderness are their domain.

The numbered cards of each kingdom or suit walk us through the blessings and challenges each landscape presents. In many ways, the aces through tens show us aspects of the mundane and the day-to-day workings of life within each realm.

THE NUMBERS AT A QUICK GLANCE

Aces: Beginning, a starting point, new opportunities, new ideas, new resources

Twos: Relationships; choices; bringing people, places, ideas and things together

Threes: Collaboration, manifestation, community, striving for balance

Fours: Structure, habits, order, building strong solid relationships and foundations

Fives: Change, consequences, chance, conflict, resolution

Sixes: Identity, nurturing, learning our place in the here and now

Sevens: Lessons in focus, patience, determination, and will

Eights: Strength, persistence, timing, hard work

Nines: Breakthroughs, battle scars, rewards, things finally coming together

Tens: Legacies, ending of cycles, completion of journeys, goals achieved

Chapter 2

TAKING THE CARDS FOR A SWIM

Let's start this section by acknowledging that you bought this deck for a reason, whether it's to deepen your spiritual practice through pathwork or to use it as a journal tool. Maybe you even bought this deck to enhance your spellcasting. Or perhaps like a lot of people, you bought this deck because the mermaids' song called your tarot self to attention and you just *had* to have this deck. Regardless of the reason, purpose, or intent for the purchase of this deck, you will inevitably read from it. In this section, you will find my five steps for doing a reading with the Mermaid Tarot. (As a word of warning, the last step is broken up into sub-steps, which will make more sense when you get there.) I highly encourage you to work your way through these steps if you are new to tarot or are not yet overly confident with your reading skills, because, practice makes perfect.

STEP ONE: SET AN INTENTION FOR YOUR READING

Before you even pick up the cards, decide what the purpose of your reading will be. Is it to solve a problem? Are you seeking an answer to a very specific question, or are you just after some general guidance? Be clear and concise. Pick only *one* thing you wish to ask of the cards. When you ask, do your best not to fall into the trap of asking passive questions that really don't have specific answers. Keep your question active so that the cards can give clear guidance. Once your intention is set, hold your question in your mind's eye. Think of it as a small mantra and keep it on repeat in the back of your mind as you move on to step two.

STEP TWO: PICK A SPREAD

A spread, in very simple terms, is how you wish to lay your card or cards out to answer your question or respond to your intention statement. If you are a tarot newbie, a simple one- to three-card spread will be more than adequate, and I have provided you with some excellent starter spreads in the back of this guidebook. If you are more experienced with the cards, you more than likely have a spread in mind.

STEP THREE: SHUFFLE, CUT, AND SPREAD

Until I entered the world of tarot, I never truly understood how shuffling a deck of cards could be such a personal act. Some people are fastidious about the direction, bend, and flow of their cards and shuffles while others, not so much. I have seen some seriously messy and unkempt decks shuffled like a tossed salad. No matter how you like to shuffle or mix your cards, I encourage you to think about doing this before you even curl your fingers around the deck and cup it in your palms: Place your deck, cards facing down in a stack in front of you. Rest your hands gently on your deck, palms down. Take three nice, deep breaths and focus on that mantra … your question. You want to bring each and every word of your question/mantra to the forefront of your mind until you can see it as a sentence. You can close your eyes for this if needed. Once you have your question crystal clear in your mind and have settled yourself into the moment, pick up your cards and start your shuffle. You will be surprised how this really quick breath-work can change the energy around your reading. Even when I am doing a reading for someone else, I ask them to do this step to settle their minds and ground their energy into the present moment.

Once you feel your shuffle is done, you now have to decide if you are going to cut your cards. Personally, I don't cut my deck, but it is a common practice that may feel organic to you and your tarot practice. Cutting your deck means separating it into stacks of two, three, or four and deciding which stack you pull your cards from to lay out your spread. If, like me, you don't feel the need to cut your cards, this is where you will spread them out. I like to fan my deck facedown in a lovely arc. Above all, know that there is no right or wrong way to do any of this; it is purely personal. But no matter how you do it, shuffle, cut and spread.

STEP FOUR: DRAW AND PLACE

Now that you have shuffled your cards and cut them or spread them you are ready to select your card or cards for your chosen spread. You will also have to decide in this step if you wish to place the cards faceup or facedown. Again this is a personal thing and there is no wrong or right way to do this step. For me, I keep my cards facedown until I am ready to read the card, even if it is only a one-card spread. So go ahead, select your cards and place them in your spread.

STEP FIVE: THE READING

Do you remember the warning I gave you at the start of this section? Well, this is where it all comes together, as this step is made up of three sub-steps. Even if you only decided to do a one-card reading, all of these steps are relevant. Each of these sub-steps walks you through a reading process. For me reading is much more than a one-size-fits-all deal. There are so many ways to interpret and contextualize the cards you draw in relation to the question you asked. Here in step five, I am giving you the three most common ways to read your cards. Just take your time through each part of step five and before you know it you will have completed your reading and taken your first swim with the mermaids.

Literally: One of the ways I recommend starting a reading is a literal interpretation of the cards themselves. By this I mean no other way to interpret them except at face value. For example, the Emperor is an old dude holding a trident looking out of the card in a bit of a ticked-off manner, or the 8 of Wands showing a mermaid dashing off toward one particular wand while seeming to forget all the others exist. Start looking at the cards with a literal eye first. Write your notes and then move on to the next step.

Intuitively: One of the best parts of tarot is using it as an intuitive tool, allowing it to slowly but surely expand your awareness and get you more in tune with your gut feelings and intuitive hits. A lot of times your intuition will tell you something completely different from the literal meaning of the cards in front of you. The images on the cards themselves may trigger something much more pressing than the general question you asked them, so take a closer look at the card or cards you have drawn and sit with them for a bit. See what bubbles up and write it down under your notes from the step above. Your writing doesn't have to make sense yet—just get it down on paper and move on to the next step.

Narrative: This step of the reading is how to combine the logical, intuitive, and traditional meanings of the card or cards you have drawn. This is also the step in which you'll want to consult the card meanings section of this book. Now you get to pull it all together. Merge the notes from your logical and intuitive interpretations with the card meanings and create the story that is the answer to your question. Remember: as you start constructing the story your cards are telling, only include information that is relevant to the question you asked. You might make a note of things that seem important to other aspects of your life as well, but keep this step focused on answering your question. Even if you only have one card, there will be a story to tell. If you have three to five cards, your story will be more compelling.

If you have drawn court cards, you now have characters to write the story around; now we have real people inside our narrative. Who are they? Write your story as a two- to three-line sentence to help you learn how the cards flow, swim, and dive together. Writing will also familiarize you with how the cards merge into one another and tell different stories with different pairings and placements. Once you have your two- to three-line sentence, you will also have your answer to your initial question.

To deepen your reading process, I encourage you to read as many other tarot books as possible in addition to everything else tarot touches on: astrology, numerology, moon studies, Pagan studies, spiritual philosophy, energy work, and so on. The more you know, the better story you will be able to write, and the clearer your answers from the cards will become.

A NOTE ON REVERSALS

Generally speaking, a reversal is a card that is drawn upside down. In a reading, one or more cards may present themselves in the reversed aspect. Upside-down or reversed cards are important; in my mind, each card should be read as it is drawn or selected. You will notice in this book a reversed meaning for each card meaning description is given to assist you in getting the full story from your cards and your reading. I encourage you to read the reversed meaning even if no upside-down card is present in your spread. You never know how the cards may be blocking, repressing, or redirecting the energy and flow of each other in your spread. To the mermaids, all information is relevant—until it is not. If you would like to know more about reversals and how to weave them into your readings seamlessly, check out my book, *Tarot Reversals for Beginners*.

Right-o, you are now set to start your journey into the heart of mer-folk territory. Take your time, be humble, and use this cultural exchange wisely. Most of all, enjoy your time under the waterline.

Notes: _____

_____

_____

_____

_____

_____

_____

_____

_____

_____

_____

_____

_____

_____

_____

_____

_____

_____

_____

_____

_____

_____

_____

Chapter 3

THE MAJOR ARCANA

*Claire: Perhaps we should
tell her the truth.*

*Jamie: We say you traveled from
another time, ye may as well convince
her ye're a mermaid.*

—Outlander Series 3, "First Wife"

The Fool

As if being born from the sea foam, a young mermaid strides onto the sandy shoreline for the very first time. Awaiting her at the water's edge is a staff and a small bag that will consist of everything she will require for her journey. Everything on land is new to her. She is and will be completely out of her element while she is out of the water. Her tail slowly morphs into a pair of legs, legs she will now have to rely on to move around for her tail is useless out of the watery elements of her home. Yet despite her situation and everything she must learn and leave behind, our young mermaid is happy, curious, and ready to explore the other world she shares the great cosmos with. One can only hope she has studied well, because this new world she now finds herself in will present her with challenges and dangers.

> *Upright:* Hold onto your fishtail—a new adventure is on its way. It is time to explore new things, places, and people. Set a course for somewhere you have never been, or start learning a new skill you know nothing about. Right now is the time to be adventurous, take a chance, and know you will have all that you require for beginning a journey into the unknown.

Reversed: It can be hard to leave the comfort of what you know to venture out into mysterious and dangerous places, even if you *really* want to. It is much easier to make excuses as to why you should never take a risk than to take it. Yet try as you might, the thrill of this risk—this new and strange experience—simply does not want to leave you alone. The pull and allure might just win out in the end.

The Magician

The currents swirl in answer to the sea witches' magic, and the glow of the fire pearl becomes strong and brighter. Her magical tools of choice are laid out on her altar, and she knows she has options. For the time being, she channels the power of the wand into the fire pearl, her face a picture of focus and concentration. She keeps her hands and mind steady so as to not break the link between her tools and her magic. Silent incarnations are chanted in her head as she lets go of what she thinks she knows to allow a new sense of knowing into her thoughts. Even the fish dance and swim to the energy of her magic, knowing that they too shall benefit from her actions.

> *Upright:* There is more at your disposal right now then you actually need, which to be honest, could be causing you a small amount of anxiety. The good news is you don't have to worry about what tool or piece of advice you use, as it will bring you a result either way. The magician says, "Make the decision. What magical tool will you use? Focus your energy on it and it alone and then allow its wisdom and guidance to plot your next step." Part of unlocking your inner magic is making a decision and allowing it to be the right one.

Reversed: Doubt is currently your worst enemy. You are letting it get the better of you and allowing it to call the shots. Instead, you need to step into your power and take back control over the decision being made about your life. Magic will happen when you put your hands firmly back on the wheel and focus your energy on an attainable result, not your fear of what might go wrong.

The High Priestess

The High Priestess sees all, though sometimes that is just as much a curse as it is a blessing. As she works alone at her altar, she understands that magic always comes with a price. When you ask the sea for something, you must give something in return.

What are you willing to give? Calypso knows that the less you give, the less you get in return. That big vision you hold deep inside of you will cost you and might even break you. Do you want it anyway?

As the goddess works, she cares not about your fears, doubts, and concerns; she already sees that which you cannot. Be careful when you summon her, because she is going to expect you to have already read the terms of the deal and will be waiting for your payment.

> *Upright:* When the High Priestess shows up in your reading, you can be assured the universe knows all your thoughts, feelings, dreams, goals, and fears. There is no hiding the truth from her, for she only deals with the energy of your soul. Don't expect her to tell you anything at all, however. She may see all, but she knows experience speaks louder than words.

Reversed: Tricks, sleight of hand, and deception won't work here. Honor the goddess with honesty and integrity or beware the gift she will bestow upon you. Everything has a cost, especially a deep, dark, hidden lie.

The Empress

Yamaya is the mother of the sea, said to have birthed the fish children into existence. Her shining Venus star is the light that helps guide them home. She is the ruler of water and all who live under its protective waves. It is her job to carry life, bring newness into the world, and keep the sacred, royal genes of her people intact. Her beauty is beyond compare, and all who know her want to be just like her. She is affectionate and compassionate but knows how to scold and discipline when the situation requires it.

She holds the conch shell of fertility, and with one song she can lay the expectant seeds of something new into your life. All she wants to know is whether you will be able to see this through from conception to birth. Will you give these seeds time to germinate and grow at their own speed and flow and bear fruit in their own time? Like all mothers, Yamaya wants you to have your heart's desires but also knows that for it to happen, you need to pledge commitment and loyalty to the possibilities she can bring.

Upright: The Empress is full of potential both literally and metaphorically. Everything she does is to bring new loving creative energy into the world. She knows what it takes to see something grow

from an idea, from something intangible to a physical, tangible thing. She understands the amount of time, energy, and commitment involved in the process of creation. Now she asks if you understand as well. Nothing worth creating will be quick and easy. It will take its toll and push you to the edge of your limits and beyond. And the Empress knows that it will all be worth it in the end.

Reversed: To follow a process means to take each step one at a time. Each step is important and if you skip one or try to rush ahead you will find you will be left with nothing but anger and resentment. You may very well have grown impatient with how things are progressing in your life. You may even think you are standing still and not moving at all. This is the time that will test your resolve and your level of commitment. Give up now if you wish, but the Empress knows that all things come in their own time—that is, right and divine time, not yours.

The Emperor

Poseidon sits on his throne surrounded by the many trinkets of his station. This is a reminder to all who come before him what he commands and what must be paid for asking his assistance. He holds the trident firmly in his hand as a reminder of his power, as he is master of all of the elements: air, fire, earth, and water. He controls the weather and the waves and is always in the process of building parts of his vast empire. He is also more than just a leader, too. As father to all mer-folk, it is his responsibility to keep all of his children safe, protected, and secure. It is on his shoulders that their happiness rests. One look at his face lets you know this is not a responsibility he takes lightly.

> *Upright:* There are things that only you and you alone can do. These are important things, and they need all your focus and concentration. You are building something sustainable in your life; some of the pieces are for you to attend to and some are not. In order to make sure you have a solid foundation on which to grow and expand your own personal empire, you must take the pieces that are your personal responsibility and attend to them. Make sure each step of the way you ground your power and sharpen your empire-building skills.

Reversed: You may be trying to shift your responsibilities on to someone else, thinking that you don't need to be an active participant in the creation of your goal or dream. You may want to reconsider that line of thinking. A leader that doesn't actually lead is weak, and a weak leader puts all under their rule in harm's way. There may very well be small meaningless tasks that are better delegated to others, but when it comes to your creation, your empire, you must mold it with your own two hands. Otherwise, all you could be left with is the crumbled mess of what could have been.

The Hierophant

Can you imagine a world with no recorded history? Nothing to tell us anything at all about how the world we live in has been shaped, molded, and grown? All those stories and their cast of colorful characters would never have been told if someone like our scribe never made a conscious effort to record them. Every generation has a story to tell, a lesson to share, and wisdom to impart. To think of a world where that information is not accessible is, well, unthinkable! The Hierophant knows more than most just how important it is to document important people, places, and events. Who we are today is a product of those stories. Without them, none of us would have any sense of identity or purpose. We would have nothing to ground us into the space and time we currently exist in.

> *Upright:* History is important. Like it or not you are a product of your history and your ancestral history all rolled up into one. This is why the Hierophant always seems to have a quill in her hand and a book under her arm. It is her job to retell the stories that shaped the rules you now live by (and you liking them is not even close to being the point). Rules are in place for a reason. History has some very important lessons. Listen, read, and learn.

Reversed: It may be time to consider writing a new chapter in an old book. Rules are meant to be challenged and changed and history is always begging to be re-written. Just make sure you have considered all the consequences before you commit to writing it down. Remember whatever you do now will affect more than just you.

The Lovers

One of the longest relationships we have in our physical incarnation is the relationship with ourselves. We spend the majority of our lives trying to reconcile the two parts that make us whole, the physical and the vibrational. Sometimes we see it as experiencing two different lives via two totally different selves. In much the same way, our young mermaid tries to envision what she would be like as a human girl with a life on land. The relationship we have with ourselves is hard, messy, and often times complicated.

Why are we here? Why in this body? Why in this family? Why [fill in the blank]? The relationship we have with ourselves serves as the baseline for all other relationships in our physical experience. Learning to deal with the duplicitous self is therefore more important than most of us truly believe.

Upright: The Lovers speaks of two energies, two pieces coming together to journey. It is a reconciliation of opposites for a more cohesive experience. This is the card of Gemini, the twin energies of the self as represented by our mermaid. Is she seeing the other part of who she is or is she seeing who she wishes to be? This is one of the many questions the Lovers raises. Do you know what your other half even looks like? Can you even identify the energy that surrounds your vibrational self, the self not tainted with ego? Making time to get to know yourself is important. Making time to love and honor yourself is part of setting the foundation for all the relationships that come next.

Reversed: What you see is what you get, or so you like to think. But is it really? Mirrors are deceptive—they don't show a true double. Instead, they reflect back to you something similar but slightly different. Whatever you see is from a different angle, flipped and shifted by a trick of the light. What you think you are seeing for yourself right now is not a true image. You're not really paying attention; you are refusing to see the difference, the skewed perspective of the real picture. This is to your detriment and all your relationships will pay the price for your lazy approach.

The Chariot

There are stories and tales from various cultures about the horse that lives under the water. Be it a water horse, seahorse, or as the Greeks called it, *hippocampus*, the stories all speak of a fast and powerful creature. For the mer-folk, the horses under the waterline are very real and part of their daily lives. They carry cargo and building materials, and ferry mer-folk from place to place. The horses are also trained to rescue those lost at sea and to deliver messages to those under the water and upon the land. Only those with a special ancestral bond can hear water horses, and only those who have the horses in their blood can train them. For everyone else, the horses under the water are strong, stubborn, and highly unpredictable.

> *Upright:* Buckle up—things are about to get interesting. The hippocampus is being prepared for a journey. Its gear is being lovingly secured and strapped into place. It is all but ready to take you where you need to be. The journey will likely be interesting, as they rarely take you where you want to go, only to the places they know you *need* to go. You might find their method liberating or frustrating depending on how deeply you are attached to your

destination. Either way, you are in for a ride you won't quickly forget.

Reversed: There are times when parts of our lives feel like they are being driven by an out-of-control beast that does not seem to have any real idea where it is going and why it needs to get us there. Instead, we find ourselves tossed about and at the mercy of the beast's powerful movement. We feel that these movements in our lives are out of control; nothing seems to make any logical sense. The chariot has run amuck. The truth, however, is that we would not have been able to ride the beast in the first place if we did not have an affinity for it. Like the water horses of legend, you have a bond with this movement and chaos. If you would only trust in your ability to steer your life, you would be able to get it back under control.

Strength

The southern right whale only has one natural predator once it is fully grown: humans. Under the waves, no one else bothers this graceful, peaceful giant. Unfortunately, they find themselves trapped year after year in human fishing lines or caught in human-made oil slicks. Today, this whale has found itself tangled and in a state of distress. Left alone and to its own devices, the whale would surely drown as it would be unable to surface to take a breath. Thankfully one of the patrolling mermaids has spotted it and is carefully untangling its body and fins from the deadly netting. As she works on freeing the whale, she sings a healing song to calm it and ease its anxiety. Gentle and nimble hands work the net and the whale's side. For its part, the whale will not forget this act of kindness, this act of someone so much smaller and frail coming to its aid.

> *Upright:* It is easy to think that big things, powerful things, don't need help and assistance. We assume their sheer size and might is all they will ever need to get them out of trouble. Isn't it easy to make a judgment call based on outside appearances alone? This sort of bias is often wrong and creates dangerous situations where we ignore those seemingly

more capable than us when we see them struggling. The truth is that everyone struggles. Everyone needs help and assistance once in a while, and it would be deeply troubling if we become desensitized to the pain and suffering of those around us because of our bias.

Reversed: There is a difference between power and strength. One is used to intimidate, manipulate, and control, while the other is about something much deeper inside of us—a vulnerable space where we can allow ourselves to tremble on shaky legs but move anyway. Right now you are confusing your deeper strength for weakness. You have convinced yourself that looking powerful is more important than looking weak. The truth is, however, that being scared and uncertain is all part of being strong. Just like the whale, you must trust that where you are now will bring the support, compassion, and kindness you need.

The Hermit

In the darkest parts of the ocean, where the bouncing rays of light from the sun never break through, the Hermit makes his rounds. In the deathly still darkness he shines his fire pearl lantern in and out of the sea caverns as he makes his way through his evening moving meditation. The chances of finding anyone or anything down here to disturb him are extremely low. Here he finds peace, and somewhat ironically, no part of him can hide. Down here in the dark dead spaces of the sea, the only thing he has to occupy himself with is him—his thoughts and everything he is still attached to. This is the perfect place to journey to the self, to find one's true voice, to find one's own burning fire pearl in the dark spaces the sunlight has forgotten.

> *Upright:* The Hermit teaches us that there is a big difference between being alone and being lonely, and we all need alone time. A time where we can find a space that is inhabited just by us. Space where nothing and nobody can disturb us. A place where the only voice we hear is our own. For as the Hermit knows only too well until we close the door, walk away and shut out the noise we cannot truly discern which part of the story is ours and which part is best left for others to play.

Reversed: In its upright position, the Hermit calls for solitude, but in the reversed position, that time alone is ending. Despite how you feel, it is time to rejoin the rest of the world. You have heard all you need to for now. Take what you have learned and use it when you return to the noise of everyday life. Your respite is now over.

Wheel of Fortune

The helm of a long forgotten vessel is home to new life at the bottom of the sea. Fish swim by as seaweed and coral repurpose the once-prized ship's wheel. The intricate markings around the wheel show that once upon a time, this ship was steered and directed by the planets that would have been clearly visible in the night sky out in the open ocean. Now both the planets and helm are out of view; advances and change have made them obsolete. We are reminded here that our purpose and roles change. Views change, and life as we know it is only temporary.

> *Upright:* What was once up will eventually find its way down. What was once lost and broken will eventually be found and given new life. The Wheel of Fortune is a reminder of the temporary nature of our physical existence. Things change, shift, and move. Nothing stays as it is forever; time marches on whether we like it or not. Where you find yourself now may not be the same in the future. Acceptable or not, it won't last so either enjoy the moment the Wheel brings you, or hold on to the hope that things won't always be this way if your situation is unacceptable.

Reversed: Try as you might, you cannot stop the Wheel from turning. Things must change. People must come and go, and situations evolve. Whether or not you *like* change is totally irrelevant when the Wheel shows up. Keep up your fight and this change will be painful; what could have been a point of joyous expansion will be a miserable journey through the muddy waters of your ego.

Justice

A set of scales under the waves between the coral may be an odd sight, perhaps pointless or even redundant. But even mer-folk culture has rules and regulations. Order and structure are just as important below the water line as above. This particular set of scales shows us something interesting, perhaps a peek into how justice is carried out in the watery world of the mer-folk. The scrolls seem to outweigh the blade. In other words, wisdom, knowledge, and mediation will always be the preferred option over violence, revenge, or acts of all-out war. There is an element of karmic justice here as well, something that has long been sought and will long be felt or an outcome that will benefit all over the long term.

> *Upright:* When the scales offer us a chance to learn something important, we should take notice. The information being presented to you right now will not only benefit you where you are but also may prove useful wherever you may find yourself in the future. The past cannot be changed; your future is being forged right now in front of the scales of karmic balance. Think carefully about what kind of world you want to live in once the problem or situation has finally been dealt with.

Reversed: Short-term gains may mean long-term pain. Do not cut off your nose to spite your face. Things may seem like they are not in your favor, but remember that justice is not about being right or avenged—it is about finding a way to reconcile an act that has already been done. Reconciliation can never truly make up for it or repair the damage that has taken place, but the longer you try and mold it to your pain, the worse off you will find yourself and everyone involved.

The Hanged Man

Looking at this image, can you tell if our merman was caught in a fishing net or if he put himself inside it? Does it even matter how he got into the net in the first place? Upside down in a net is where he is, and by the look of him, he is no hurry to remove himself from his hanging position. With his spiky hair just inches from the dock, he looks out from the net with a bit of cheeky expression on his face, as if he knows something you don't, or as if he has found the very thing you keep searching for.

> *Upright:* Despite the appearance of your current set of circumstances, the Hanged Man wants you to let go and surrender. He asks you to stop trying to control the outcome, to stop fighting what is and detach yourself just for a little while. You'll see that what you want to happen can't while you are in the way. It might hurt your pride to hear, but it's time to sit down, shut up, and let the universe drive for a while.

Reversed: You may have had your hands off the wheel of your life for a little too long. Things sorted themselves out ages ago, but you forgot to get down from your hook and rejoin your life. It's time to get your head back in the game, dear one, as the universe has served you up some goodies. Now, you have to take those goodies and do something with them.

Death

As above, so below. What happens on the surface of the ocean has a deep and profound effect under the water. Pollution and human expansion have done more than its fair share of harm. Yet just as above, under the waves are caretakers and rescuers amongst the mer-folk, and they work just as tirelessly as their fin-free human friends. The irony is that both need each other in times of crises. In other words, when Death comes knocking, it comes knocking at both doors at the same time. Sometimes those who stand in Death's way can be rescued and healed. Sometimes they cannot. Regardless of the danger, risk, and the putrid mess Death leaves behind in its wake, there will always be those who will risk themselves so others can have a chance to start again.

> *Upright:* Death always leaves behind something to clean up. Like it or not, the sludge that seems to stick to your skin and seeps into your lungs is the residue of Death's deeds and it needs to be cleaned. Just like the ocean animals in this card, you may need someone to help you with this process. Seek those who work on cleaning, clearing, and healing the energy left behind from old cycles. Let them assist you in leaving behind that which makes you

weak and vulnerable and allow them to restore and strengthen you. These may be friends, family members, or spiritual teachers—don't rule anyone out, just ask for assistance and allow it to appear.

Reversed: You may think you can do this alone, but the truth is you can't. Sure, you could wallow in your disintegrating mess for a while, but you won't be able to stay there. At some point, you will have to get up and get on with life, which means you will need help, support, and someone to assist you in finding a new normal. Like it or not, you just aren't the same as you were before Death came knocking on your door.

Temperance

Under the power of the solar eclipse, the potions master mixes her most powerful potion yet. Timing is everything—the wrong move or amount will change the entire potion. The ingredients she is using have been carefully researched, hand-picked, and measured three times before being blended carefully, timed precisely to when the moon begins its journey between the sun and the earth. Every single detail plays a part in the potion Temperance now makes, which is why it must also be mixed above the waterline as the chemical reaction it will have with the atmosphere above the water is crucial to the potion's success. But just what is Temperance mixing? What will this potion do once it is complete? We will know only once it is finished brewing, and Temperance is not yet at that stage. She is still very much in the act of doing, of blending and balancing.

> *Upright:* Temperance finds herself in such an interesting position in the major arcana, and it is her position that is key to understanding her full power. Temperance sits between Death and the Devil, a bridge between the old self and the new. She receives you after your ego has passed through Death's door and shows you the possibilities of

what life could be like by introducing you to the Devil. It is not her place to cast judgment or to even make suggestions for how you should proceed from this point forward. If anything, Temperance is more interested in showing, not telling. For this reason, it is so important you pay close attention to everything she does while you are in her presence. Watch how she creates. Study her guided and extremely thought-out actions. When you watch, maybe you will not be as tempted when she hands you over to the step that comes next.

Reversed: When you are out of step with Temperance or have failed to fully engage in your time with her, you may notice that all the timed events of your life are a little off. Nothing seems to line up. People in your life keep missing each other. Places you want to go seem to always be out of reach, and things you want never seem to coincide with your flow of abundance. Everything just feels out of step, out of sync, missing some crucial piece of information. Perhaps next time you will pay better attention to Temperance and her ways.

The Devil

We have all been guilty of chasing pretty, sparkly things. We have all spent time desiring and plotting how to get our hands on the latest and greatest shiny thing. We have all allowed our desire to trap us and make us prisoners of consumerism. Things are seductive. Having things makes us feel useful, needed, and part of the material world we live in. Even the mermaids are guilty of chasing things they could really live without and don't really have a use for, and every so often one of them finds their way into a real trap. Taking a closer look, you will see that like most traps of desire, there is no lock. The mermaid can leave anytime she wants, yet she is still staring at the treasures in front of her as if dazed and held captive by nothing more than her unchecked need.

Upright: The Devil always leaves the door open, the locks unlocked, and the exit clearly marked. Yet surprisingly, many people never seem to make their way out of the desire den. It *is* pretty spectacular: you can have whatever you want whenever you want, and no one is ever going to judge you. It's almost as if you are amongst friends. All the while, the Devil simply holds the space for you to explore all your desires. He doesn't judge, he doesn't

humiliate…he doesn't really do anything. He leaves all the action to you. So what will you do? Be like the mermaid and continue being trapped or open the door and move onto other things away from all that glitters, sparkles, and calls your name?

Reversed: At some point, the mermaid will have to make her way out of that trap. She can't stay there, and whoever laid the trap for her knows she won't survive in it, hence why it is not locked. She will eventually come to her senses and realize that her life is more important than the things she has chased onto the beach. Her mind will clear, and she will make her way back to the sea. You too have had a moment of clarity, and although it isn't easy to say goodbye to something or someone you have pined after, you know it is the best thing you could ever do.

The Tower

Before an earthquake is a low humming vibration that all animals seem able to feel. This hum alerts sentient beings to incoming danger and allows them time to find somewhere safer to be. No mer-folk can be found in our card here—they have fled, instinctively sensing a need to move as the buildings crumble and fall onto empty streets below. Earthquakes are an inevitable part of living on a constantly moving and shifting planet. Suffering because of it is optional, however. The mer-folk know which things in their lives can be rebuilt and which cannot. Can you say the same?

> *Upright:* The Tower reminds us that things fall down and break apart, especially things that are built on rocky foundations or near emotional and mental fault lines. Destruction is a fact of life—none of us escape it. Things end, crumble, and disintegrate right in front of our eyes all throughout our lives. For whatever reason, you have forgotten that everything is temporary. Something in your life needs to be rebuilt or replaced. Its current construction no longer serves its purpose, and it is being destroyed. This is a good thing and necessary for something new to find its way into your life.

Reversed: If the upright version of this card implies an external break down, then the reversed aspect could very well indicate an internal blowout. Stress, anxiety, and resistance wreak havoc on the body. Be mindful of how your body is communicating to you right now, as it may very well be sending you warning signs that things are not as they should be and trouble is on the horizon. The trouble could be a weakened immune system, stress-related headaches, digestive issues, or other explosive bodily functions.

The Star

Some wishes vibrate so strongly that they never have to be spoken out loud. These wishes are carried on the breeze, and become tossed and churned over the waves and eventually mix with the rhythm of the sea foam. The Dreamweaver hears the sea foam's song and catches the melody in her magical conch shell. Under the watchful gaze of the evening star, the Dreamweaver plays the conch shell in a tune filled with the hearts desires of all those who hold a special wish in their hearts, sending it back to the universe as a wish fulfilled.

> *Upright:* That big dream, wish, or goal—the one that scares you so much that you won't even allow yourself to think about it for longer than a second—is screaming at the top of its lungs. Your heart is talking to the universe, and the Dreamweaver is listening. Sometimes our biggest and scariest dreams, wishes, and goals are part of our karmic journey. They will come to pass whether we believe we deserve them or not. Now is one of those times. Your heart is setting the course of your next adventure, and the Dreamweaver has answered its call.

Reversed: You are not clear on what you want, and it seems like you are doing nothing but chasing your own tail. In order for the Dreamweaver to hear the beat of your wish's heart, you need to focus, be still, and make a decision. There cannot be forward movement or progress until you know the direction in which you wish to go. Stop the noise, go within, and allow your heart to beat clearly and loudly.

The Moon

You may think you know all about the siren and her song. You may even think that you know all there is to know about her story, but you may be wrong. Those who have been blessed with the gift of song belong to certain groups: there are healing sirens, dream sirens, warning sirens, and nightmare sirens, just to name a few. The healing sirens sing only under the light of the full moon, when they raise their voices across the ocean to the sky they sing a healing chant, sending out wave after wave of healing frequencies. These frequencies help with calming the world's tensions, restoring balance and sending relief to those who are suffering. The full moon siren also does one other unique thing her fellow sirens do not—she calls lost souls home. All those who were lost at sea and wandering the waves she calls home with the vibration of her melody. All this happens in one night, the only night of the month when the moon is completely full.

Upright: Have you ever walked the shoreline under the full moon and watched as the moonbeams dance and sway within the rolling waves only to disappear once they hit shore? It's like watching a magical underwater light show. If you watch from a certain angle, the waves look alive. The truth is that they are simply answering the siren's song, spreading her energy and carrying her frequencies to all. Under the light of the moon, it looks so spectacular, yet what happens under the blanket of darkness looks very different from what happens in broad daylight. In the dark we find more space for our imaginations to run wild, allowing us to lose all sense of perception and see things that would not be visible under the sun's intense rays.

Reversed: Are you scared of the dark? Many people resist looking into the darkness, scared of what they might find, the sounds they hear. Noise behaves differently at night and can make you believe things that aren't true, which might be why you are currently hiding under the covers, waiting for the light to return. The problem is that night falls every twenty-four hours, so you are eventually going to have to take a look around and see what exactly has you so spooked.

The Sun

The sun illuminates the water under the sea, forming bubbles of golden light. Young mer-children hold out their hands as if trying to catch the light in the palms of their hands. As the light bounces around the rippling currents of the ocean, even the sea turtles bask in its warm rays. In the shallower parts of the ocean, the sun acts much the same as it does above the waterline, bringing life to plants and allowing coral and sea vegetables to grow and thrive. The warmer waters often provide safe spaces and sanctuaries to sea life and the mer-folk alike. Here under the glow of the midday sun, you can relax and play, and forget about your worries. If you are lucky, you might even catch one of those golden bubbles of liquid sunlight.

> *Upright:* The Sun gives life. It provides energy and warmth for things to grow and thrive. It is one of the key elements of creation along with water and oxygen, which in the shallow, warm waters of the sea are all abundance. Here are the perfect conditions for creation, an auspicious merging of energy provides the exact conditions you need to solve a problem, begin a relationship, or start a new project.

Reversed: Just as the Sun can give life, it can also take it away. Climate change has shown the devastating effects of the Sun on bleached and dying coral reefs all over the world. What were once thriving feeding and spawning areas now lay barren like underwater ghost towns. We are reminded that the Sun is a power we don't have control over. When it is done providing life-giving support, you will know it—it will start to burn through all it has created in search of something more worthy of its time and immense energy. Let this be a warning to not linger too long in the heat of this card. Use it for what you need. Respect and honor its creation power. Then release it before it turns on you and burns everything you love to cinders.

Judgment

The shaman of rebirth plays the ancient song of release through his conch shell, filling the water with waves of forgiveness. To those with open hearts, the song releases them from their binding bubble and allows them to swim free. It is only those who feel worthy to drop their burdens that find themselves reborn, new and ready to start again. Those who feel their sins are too heavy or too large to forgive will stay trapped in the suffering of their own creation. Thankfully, the shaman will play again, always offering an opportunity for liberation and rebirth.

> *Upright:* How do you work with the energy of Judgment? Are you free and easy with how you dish it out, in turn allowing others to do the same when it comes to judging you? Or are you forgiving, compassionate, and understanding, exactly how you would want others to be if you found yourself on the other side of a judgment-filled glare? Judgment is a mindset more than anything. It is a standard we have set for how we decided what actions are good and what actions are bad. In turn, Judgment leads us to decide how actions should or should not be punished.

Everything seems fine until you fall prey to your own rules. Think carefully about how you deal with Judgment today—maybe in this instance you can be the shaman and help release someone else from their burden of guilt and shame.

Reversed: It may seem like fun to be someone else's judge and jury, but it doesn't feel as fun when someone else does it to you. Judgment is a binding energy; it matters not if you are the one being judged or doing the judging. It creates a small, isolated space of shame, pain, and guilt. The action of judgment then undermines all the good and potential good the person being judged has done and will do. Just remember that while you have fun pointing your finger and smirking from your pedestal, that one day you too will be at the mercy of the shaman of rebirth.

The World

We all come from water. Above the waterline or below it, none of us here on the planet we have named earth would survive without it. Water is one of the fundamental requirements of life. We are conceived in water, can be born in water, and can die in water. Water represents the ultimate cycle of life, both the beginning and the end. Even ashes end up flowing back to be one with the water. The water is us and we are the water. If we flow clear and pure, so too will the water. Mother, guardian, creator, within you, all is as it shall be and with you, all that could be will be.

Upright: The World card reminds us of the cyclic nature of existence. Where something ends, something else begins. We all end and begin in the same place; ultimately, we never go anywhere. Something in your life may have come to a natural end, but it is not the end you need to be focused on. It is what has been created because something has come full circle.

Reversed: Distractions, delays, and the road less taken have all brought you so close, yet so far from where you need to be. You may think you have everything you need to finally finish what you started or end

something that you feel has outlived its usefulness but the universe wants you to think again. Things are not where they need to be for you to close out this experience, situation, problem, or relationship. There is still work to do and you must keep going. The good news, of course, is that the end is in sight.

Chapter 4

THE MINOR ARCANA

"I must be a mermaid, Rango.
I have no fear of depths and a great
fear of shallow living."

—Anaïs Nin

THE SUIT OF
Cups

Ace of Cups

Under the sea, cups seem out of place. They merely look like they need to be filled, and as we can see with our Ace of Cups, this one has been converted into someone's home. It is filled to the brim with the magic and miracle of life. Someone saw this cup as an opportunity for expansion and a new life and jumped right in it, literally. It is interesting that without even knowing what its true purpose was, the sea took the cup in and used it to its fullest potential anyway. Now it is a part of the living landscape, another piece of the larger puzzle of life under the sea.

> *Upright:* Are you using a gift to its fullest potential or do you have it on a shelf somewhere while you try and figure out what it is? The Ace of Cups lets you know that if it has shown up, the conditions are already there for it to fulfill its true purpose. Trying to understand it is not the same as actually using it. Cups are a feeling suit which is why logic and reason are not always the best way to deal with them. I suggest you better make use of what has presented itself before someone else comes along and claims it.

Reversed: Instead of seeing opportunity there is a good chance you are seeing burden, which means you are more than happy to leave your cup upside down for now. You may not feel ready to deal with turning it upright and finding out what's inside it—or more to the point, what its spaciousness offers. And that is perfectly fine as long as you don't wait too long for that cup won't be around forever.

2 of Cups

Do you remember that feeling of excitement mixed with anxiety that happens when you meet someone new, someone you simply gel with? That feeling like nothing and nobody could come between the spark that the two of you have created. This feeling doesn't always mean love, nor does it always last long term. What it does mean, is that right now you have met someone who seems to excite you. Just for now forget about what comes next and don't get too caught up in what if's, instead, just allow yourself to enjoy how you are feeling in this moment because the two of you are coming together for a reason.

Upright: The 2 of Cups heralds a meeting. Someone new is coming into your life, who shares similar thoughts, feelings and beliefs. This may be a romantic opportunity, or it could be a chance to find a new friend. Either way, a new and beneficial relationship is swimming into your life, so raise a cup and celebrate.

Reversed: Are you resisting bringing a new person into your life? When this card shows up reversed, it indicates that you might still be holding on to

past hurts. Someone in your past has caused you pain and you are letting it get in the way of forming a new relationship. This could be romantic in nature or it could be a fabulous new friend that has the potential to expand your life if only you would give them a chance.

3 of Cups

The art of imitation is a fun way to put yourself in the shoes of someone else. Here in the 3 of Cups, our little mermaids are playing out what they believe to be a human ritual, the tea party. They raise their cups and make up a toast before they laugh at how this strange ceremony makes them feel. But that's the thing about friends—you can be silly and act out funny scenes just for the sheer joy of it. Our little mermaids don't really understand the need for cups and teapots, but the play itself brings them closer to each other and keeps them in the vibration of happiness.

Upright: As social beings, we need time with others. To keep our emotional, physical, and mental bodies balanced, we need to socially interact with people who make us laugh and understand us. This interaction can be as simple as having a cup of tea or as complex as playing out a scene in a movie you have all seen a million times. This social engagement will increase your spiral of abundance, boost your energy, and promote the vibration of joy throughout your cells.

Reversed: Now is not the time to close yourself off from others. If anything now is the time you need your friends the most. Shutting down and trying to go it alone is very rarely the answer to anything. If you are not doing things to increase your levels of joy and keep your mind clear, you are not maintaining proper self-care. Sure, it seems easier to hide in a cave and continue to be miserable, but some social time will actually improve your mood and help you solve a problem you have been struggling with.

4 of Cups

Although it may look like the human has spent the night drowning his sorrows, we can't be sure that is actually what happened. The mermaid behind him gives us a hint at a different story. Perhaps the scene we have stumbled onto in the 4 of Cups is more about the emptiness of excess. The young mermaid who only wants to be noticed offers up what she believes the man she has been following wants. The problem is, if the three cups in front of him have failed to bring him any emotional reward, then what is the point of accepting the fourth cup? How can more of the same pull him out of his slump? Perhaps it is not the cups themselves that are the problem but what is inside of them and if that is the case, then perhaps the mermaid has something very different to offer. But until the Man engages his peripheral vision he may never see her. Instead, she and all she offers will merely be a shadow lurking somewhere in the corner of his eye.

> *Upright:* Sometimes getting everything you want doesn't feel like you dreamed it would. Sometimes it is just too much, too overwhelming, and too good to be true. The bigger problem, of course, is that once you are finally manifesting what you

want, everyone wants to give you more of the same. Sometimes you have to be very careful what you wish for … because it might just show up.

Reversed: Do you know what is on the other side of boredom? Most people don't know how to answer that question because they never break through to the other side. Instead, they feed their monkey mind to rid themselves of boredom. Yet there is something to be said about going deeper, about not giving into the emotions that plague the mind and allowing oneself to fully explore why we feel bored, overwhelmed or even pity. There is a point beyond the boredom when the mind is finally quiet and still, a moment when a magical mermaid can come along and offer you the most magical gift. If you want to get there, you must first release your need to feed your emotions.

5 of Cups

Saying goodbye is never easy; letting go is harder still, but not all creatures find joy in the same place which is something our Selkie is finding out. Her best friend is returning to the sea—life on land is just not for her. The path they once walked together is now going to divide into two different directions: one on land, the other out at sea. Personal destiny is just that, personal. But that doesn't make it any less painful to accept that it might mean saying goodbye to those you love.

> *Upright:* There is no pleasant way to experience the 5 of Cups—it is one of those cards that will bring a certain level of pain with it. We are reminded here that life is not without choices, and choices are not without consequences. The 5 of Cups reminds us that pain is a part of life, but suffering is optional. Fabulous new opportunities await you after you say goodbye. Life will go on, and this won't be the last time you will have to let something or someone go.

> *Reversed:* You can't keep things as they are yet expect everything to change. Holding on to what you have with one hand while trying to grasp onto what you

want with the other just won't work—something has to give. Use this time to take a good look at your current situation and ask the hard question; what are you willing to let go of now to have what your heart desires in the future?

6 of Cups

Oh, the joy of finding new things to play with and explore, especially when you have no idea what the object you found is actually used for. Mermaid children play freely without the knowledge of what their playthings are, and none of them care. Their "right now" experience is unrestricted, not bogged down with meaning. It is merely a time to be silly and creative, and let their imaginations run wild. You may recognize the found objects in this card as cups, but that is only because you have a memory associated with what a cup is. When you were a child, someone showed you a cup, told you what its name was, and explained what it was for. Someone else's meaning then became your own, and the objects now known as "cups" came to have a shared story. The mermaid children do not share your story. They do not have a passed-down narrative to explain cups and therefore are just free to explore them however they wish.

Upright: The 6 of Cups brings into focus stories of your childhood, stories that perhaps were never truly yours. Maybe they were told to you as a way of molding your engagement and interaction with the world around you. Right now, however, that story doesn't feel the way it once did. Just like the

mer-children, you are aching to write a new story, one that is yours and yours alone. Free from the rules that someone else once explained to you. Free of someone else's meaning.

Reversed: Memories are deceptive, especially ones from childhood. If you have siblings, you will know only too well how differently you and siblings remember specific events from your childhood. What may have been painful and uncomfortable for you may have been joyful and exciting to one of your family members. Then again, you don't need an extended family to have experienced the difference in a shared memory. With the 6 of Cups in reverse, you are being asked to re-evaluate one or two of your childhood memories that seem to be triggering you emotionally. It is time to un-hook yourself from the story of the child self and re-write it for the adult self to experience.

7 of Cups

It is easy to allow yourself to get distracted by whatever shiny new thing just happens to roll on by. Even under the sea treasures can be irresistible. In fact just looking for new sparkly items can be a full-time job. It can take up so much time that you forget to focus on all the other things in your life and before you know it all you have in your life are vessels filled with lackluster, useless, discarded bits and pieces.

> *Upright:* Distractions are a part of everyday life. It is easy to allow them to take control and dictate the terms of your day. It takes strength and commitment, however, to turn away from them and keep your emotions and mind clear and focused. Allowing yourself to fill your days with what seems like busyness doesn't mean you are actually achieving anything, except maybe cluttering up your mental, emotional, and vibrational space. So for now, leave the shiny objects where you found them and leave the space for something you really wish to experience.

Reversed: Congratulations, one of your shiny objects led you to something exciting and engaging. The real lesson here is that you took action and didn't simply move onto the next shiny thing that crossed your path. Instead, you saw something through from beginning to end.

8 of Cups

Things that seemed like a good idea at the time may not be sustainable over an extended period of time, like our two lovers in the 8 of Cups. The relationship in its current form won't make it over the long term. It might have seemed like love would conquer all, but the light of the full moon illuminates the reality of the situation. These two come from two different worlds and dream of two different futures. In order for our mermaid to stay true to herself, she is going to have to let go of her human lover and leave him sleeping on the shore to wonder if it all had just been a dream.

> *Upright:* It is not easy to admit that something you have invested time into just won't work. Walking away can be painful. Unfortunately, the problem is that if you don't walk away now, you will only make it worse when everything eventually comes crashing down on top of you. Staying will only bring you sustained pain. Leaving will hurt, but the pain will only be temporary.

Reversed: No matter what circumstance, situation, or problem you are trying to leave behind, just know that where you go, you also take yourself. In order to make sure you don't make this mistake again, you have to deal with the constant in the equation—you. Get clear on what you want so you don't have to go through this pain again.

9 of Cups

The sea witch hums a long-lost sea shanty as she spins and stirs the bubbling concoction in the nine cups before her. The sun, which was hanging in the middle of the sky when she began casting her spell, has now sunk into the darkness of the ocean, leaving the illuminated magic she creates as the only light. The shanty she sings brings a smile to her face as it reminds her of a time when she was an adventurous and mischievous mermaid. It is this energy that she slowly but surely embeds into her brew. Enchanting each and every cup with the potential for joy, love, and wonder. But who shall drink from these cups? Only the sea witch knows. She seeks those with a spark of spontaneity and a flare of recklessness but who walk with a compassionate core.

Upright: If the sea witch has blessed you with one of her cups, congratulations. Only one who is filled with gratitude and has an open heart can drink one of her magic brews. Only the person who sees others success as their own will be able to create true success for themselves. It takes someone special to see that when others do well, we all do well. To see that blessings grow when they are honored and to be humble enough to accept the gifts that now come their way.

Reversed: Not all agree with the sea witch's magic. Not all believe she and she alone should be able to select who does and does not get to sip from her magical cups. Such figures lurk in the caverns and caves surrounding her workspace, oozing with jealousy and resentment while their mouths chant the "why not me" mantra. These shadow dwellers take no joy in other peoples' blessings and are instead steeped in a state of perpetual ego envy. Eventually, their lack of gratitude will cause them to shrivel and dull, leaving them nothing but misery and despair.

10 of Cups

What could be more mundane and domestic then grocery shopping at the local farmers' market? Then again, what could be more magical and grounding then doing everyday tasks outside in the open?

Upright: The 10 of Cups speaks of the need to ground emotional energy back into the world of the everyday, the boring process called life, settling your weary emotions into the habitual patterns of domesticity. It is here, in the basic grind of life that we truly find flow. It is in the mundane that we get lost and leave our stress and drama behind. It is this energy that now beckons you to calm, relax, and allow yourself to once again get swept up in everyday tasks that comprise a life with purpose and meaning.

Reversed: Have you ever felt like you didn't belong? Like somehow you were in the wrong place at the wrong time? When our emotions are not grounded, it is easy to feel like where we are is the last place we are meant to be, so we allow ourselves to imagine somewhere better. We fill our minds with

expectation and become even more emotionally off balance as we detach more from our daily lives and attach instead to illusion, to distractions. The problem is that to create any dream and bring any fantasy to life, we must first be grounded in the moment we are currently in—even the place you think you need to escape. Although the paradox of manifestation is real, the suffering your upside-down 10 of Cups brings doesn't have to be.

The Page of Cups

A page sits on the beach trying his best to practice his scrying, but it sure is hard to see the images inside the water his cup holds when there's a fish jumping around in it. Then again, it might just be part of the lesson. Lots of things move around in the water and he will have to learn to be able to see past them, through them, to the important information he seeks. So what better way to start your scrying lesson than with a fish in your cup, something to assist you in seeing past the ripples life creates, talking you through the process of the currents of life, showing you how to look deeper, further, and with more meaning to all that is being offered to you.

> *Upright:* Have you been feeling like you need to settle your emotions? Like perhaps you might need to ground yourself back into your body and feel more engaged in what is going on in your life? The Page of Cups and his little fish are here to help. They want to assist you in focusing and drawing your energy back to the present moment, where it will help you start something new. Things may seem to be jumping all over the place at the moment, but like the fish in the cup, they are only a distraction, something trying to teach you how to steady your emotions, control your mind and ground your body.

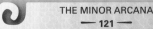

Reversed: The Page of Cups has a tendency to be moody and disengaged when upside down. The emotions have won out, and the page has given up even trying to move past his or her brooding. This may be an important part of the page's learning how to master those stormy emotions, learning how to feel it all. With time, the page will learn to harness this sort of moodiness. For now, he or she just sits in it, stewing and sorting.

The Knight of Cups

Leaning over the chalice as if it were a loving friend, the Knight of Cups gazes into the water the chalice holds as if seeking something, perhaps a sign. Maybe he is a master scryer and has the ability to read beyond his reflection in the water. His blond locks caress his temples as he concentrates on nothing but what is inside of this chalice. Then again, maybe I am giving him far too much credit—let's face it, it is not beyond this knight to get lost in his own reflection and forget the rest of the world exists.

> *Upright:* The Knight of Cups is a hopeless romantic. Moments of solitude and internal reflection are not done as often as you would think when it comes to spiritual expansion. This knight *definitely* loves to indulge in this own fantasy world, one he has constructed to fit his version of the world he wishes to live in—I am not saying there is anything wrong with that. Truthfully, however, it is very hard to focus on the here and now when the mind is attached to a moment that doesn't exist. Fantasy has its place, but illusions and delusion are dangerous and can cause more harm than good.

Reversed: It is not uncommon for this knight to suffer from depression, especially when he realizes that the harsh reality of his world is closing in fast and eating away at the fantasy he has created. Melancholy and sullenness are indicators that this knight is no longer in control of his emotional well-being.

The Queen of Cups

In the beginning, was a goddess, Nammu, through whom all things were made. From the sea, she birthed the heavens so she could look at the stars. As the goddess settled into her watery home, she knew the world that she had created would be constant work, never truly complete and always in need of new and exciting creations. Each year Nammu swirls her magical chalice and gives life to more of the world. Her sea-encrusted crown concentrates her power and allows her to see creation within her mind's eye first and then feel it like a living thing as it makes its way through her fingertips. As her power infuses the sea water from her chalice, it bubbles and foams, rising up out of the depths of the ocean and into the air above where it is transported across the waves and on the breeze to create the vision that once, only the goddess could see.

Upright: Life force energy flows. It moves through all living things like a wave. Sometimes it is gentle and calm, and other times it is crashing against us like it is trying to propel us out of our bodies. The Queen of Cups has a few tricks up her sleeve—or, more to the point, in her cup—to teach you about how to deal with this ever-flowing energy. She wants to tap you into your intuitive feeling center and show you how to work the controls. She knows that if you learn her lesson well, you won't find yourself wrecked along the rocks anymore.

Reversed: It is easy to feel overwhelmed and at the mercy of your creative potential rather than liberated by it. The feelings and emotions required to harness creative energy can be difficult to control, and if you don't know how to ride the waves they create, you could find yourself pulled under by the unforgiving undertow. Hold onto the queen's cup and wait for it to right itself. Using the cup as your own personal life preserver, you will eventually find yourself back on dry land feeling a lot less panicked and out of control.

The King of Cups

A good king knows how to distinguish between emotionally charged words and genuine action. He knows how to observe and get the full picture of any and all situations, problems, or conflicts. King Triton is a master at getting below his emotions, below his ego and seeing what is truly there. He is the keeper of stories, a messenger, and herald, making it vitally important that he does not spread inaccurate information. This is why he holds his cup close to him, so he can keep his eye on what is really unfolding. Inside of his bubbling cup is a view into all the goings on inside his kingdom. Nothing and nobody escapes his attention. Using the power of his intuition, Triton is able to ascertain quickly and effortlessly where his focus needs to be. You cannot come before this king and be untrue. He already knows your truth. Instead, seek the wisdom he has to offer and let him tell you what he sees for you inside of his cup.

Upright: The King of Cups represents the highest form of emotional mastery. He has transcended above the need to simply react; instead, his calming energy is usually enough to unnerve those who come before him. He knows what it means to be a true

heart-centered leader and understands that not everyone is at the same stage of their emotional journeys. He is patient and kind most of the time, and is able to make a decision with a clear head and positive heart. These are keys to the lessons he now brings to you. It is time to put your ego aside, clear your emotional attachments and make clear, honest, heart-based decisions about the direction your life now takes.

Reversed: Generally speaking, the King of Cups is a pretty calm guy, but he does have his moods. Usually when he lashes out, it is because his patience has run out or someone is deliberately trying to deceive him. If he is continually drained he will snap and it won't be good for those involved. Perhaps it is instead best to give the king space—time to rest and rejuvenate. Better that he moves past his current state than continually be poked and prodded into conflict.

THE SUIT OF
Wands

Ace of Wands

When something is new, it has a certain spark, heat, and energy to it that lights you up. It gets you excited and seems to stream energy right into your veins. This is the gift of the Ace of Wands. This card is full of creative fire and passion, and has that lovely "new" smell about it. But before you go grab that wand and gaze into the fire pearl, think about what this new energy will change in your life. Are you ready for things to get intense, heated, and desire-driven? If so, then by all means reach in and grab that wand with all your might. If not, let it go for now. It will still be there if and when you change your mind.

> *Upright:* The Ace of Wands brings a flash of inspiration, a charge of energy and a new lease on life. This energy is not to be taken lightly. Wands are intense, charged up and ready to go now. The fire pearl on top of the wand holds great power, and with it comes the need for you to show up and be accounted for. Get ready for things to get interesting.

Reversed: If you aren't expressing your pent-up creative energy, where is it going? The energy of the Ace of Wands can be productive or destructive; it matters not to the ace. It has no predisposed position on which way you use its energy. Think about it this way, though: wouldn't life be easier if you were making things more magical rather than constantly lighting fires everywhere you go?

2 of Wands

The mer-warrior is at his station checking on the conditions around him. It is his job to keep watch because conditions in his environment can and do change quickly. He considers this sort of awareness part of his spiritual practice, for when change comes (which it will), he will be ready. He will know what direction to go and what will be required of him. Can you say the same? How aware are you about your changing environment? When working with creative energy, it behooves us to also raise our level of awareness so we can correct course when and where it is needed.

> *Upright:* You have felt the power and energy of the wands, but now you are discovering that it comes with a high level of risk. Now you have a choice to make: will you rise to the occasion and take this new adventure or idea to the next level? Or will you take your current buzz and be satisfied with the small rush the Ace of Wands gave you? Just know that if you decide to take a risk, you will have to be like the mer-warrior and step into the energy as if it was a spiritual practice, full of devotion and honor.

Reversed: After the initial rush of the energy of the Ace of Wands, you now suddenly feel like you are going nowhere fast. You could feel this way because you have decided that what you desire is not at all what you expected; let's face it, you have no desire to put your neck on the line to get what you want.

3 of Wands

This mermaid is doing something that may seem inconsequential to most, but that magnifying glass allows her to do something special. With her three wands for support, she can now take a closer look at what she has created. It is one thing to create blindly, just wishing things into creation; it is quite another to be aware and in the know about what you are creating and at what stage of the process your creations are. What better way is there to do that than with three magical wands and a magnifying glass.

> *Upright:* The 3 of Wands seems less about doing and more about observing. When you have a lot going on, it is important to take time out and check on things. The three wands can indicate a check in on three of your life pillars: love, health, and wealth. Are these areas of your life all going the way you want? Have you successfully manifested the things you want in each of these areas, or is there still work to be done? You will only know this if you are willing to take a closer look.

Reversed: Running around life with blinders on won't make the bad go away. Instead, try to see what is really happening and ask for help if you find you are in over your head. There is nothing wrong with seeking assistance. In fact, the number 3 energy of this card urges you to seek the wisdom of others.

4 of Wands

It's good when things come together. You can relax and stop to enjoy life's small, finer moments: a beautiful full moon over a volcano, the gentle breath of your lover as she or he slowly melts into your side. Moments like these, quiet snippets of completion are why we dream and have goals. This card is about the moment before the big event, the reflective part of the fire where you can take a moment to gaze at all that you have done thus far.

> *Upright:* The four wands that form a square offer you strength and stability. Your manifesting has paid off and things are finally coming together. This card brings with it the first sightings of results, the prizes in the physical world you have been slowly creating in your inner world. By taking a moment to absorb this small but significant phase, you allow yourself to create even more of what you already have.

Reversed: Why are you not allowing yourself to take a break? By rushing now, you could very well ruin the strong structure you have built. Pushing and scheming with the fiery energy of the wands won't bring your dreams and goals to you any faster; if anything, it will delay them.

5 of Wands

Power is such an interesting thing. When you have everyone on the same page and focused on the same goal, power is magnified and can create miraculous things. But when it is not structured and is instead haphazard, it can be absolutely disastrous. Thank goodness all of these mer-warriors are channeling their fire pearls toward the same target, as together they truly will be a force to be reckoned with. They also understand that containing that amount of energy takes incredible discipline—one false move or lapse in concentration and they could all be in serious danger.

> *Upright:* The 5 of Wands brings with it a promise of greatness, but whether or not things turn out to be a great success or a great debacle is really up to you. What will you do with the power that is currently being offered to you by the five wands? You have within your reach the energy and magic you need to bring that goal or dream even closer. Just know you cannot allow yourself to get flustered or sidetracked or you could blow it all up.

Reversed: Thankfully, you have some time to get all of those fire pearls in order. Right now, energy is not at full capacity, and your thoughts are in disarray. Before you work on turning this card around, get your thoughts together and focus. Remember that this card brings with it no promises or guaranteed results—it merely offers power.

6 of Wands

People crowd the night bazaar just to get a glimpse of the talented and handsome young fire pearl eater. They watch in awe and wonder at his skill and technique. They cheer at the end of each act, showing their ongoing support for his death-defying tricks. Our young fire pearl eater knows that each and every night, his applause means victory over his fear. If for one second he stopped to think about the dangers of what he was doing while doing it, he would surely be burned from the inside out.

Upright: Risks and rewards seem to go hand in hand. The bigger the risk, the bigger the reward, but success can only happen when one's thoughts and actions are aligned. There is no place for doubt or disbelief in the victor's circle.

Reversed: In order to have success, one must first be able to acknowledge others' success. That acknowledgment must be done without attachment and without judgment, for the moment one starts to attach themselves to what others have achieved is the moment one lets doubt creep in. Right now,

you are in the act of comparison and it is doing a bang-up job on your confidence levels. Don't look at what others have done—instead, focus on why you are taking this risk in the first place.

7 of Wands

Curiosity is a double-edged blade: It can bring us to places we never knew existed, and it can also … bring us to places we never knew existed. Yes, you read that correctly. Sometimes we find welcoming and inviting new playgrounds in which to explore, but other times we find ourselves trespassing. Our diver can't believe what he has found: he has just stumbled across a real mer-folk village—and he is far from being a welcome guest. The trick is to know when to stay and when to go willingly. Perhaps this is how curiosity killed the cat?

> *Upright:* You would do well to tread carefully right now, as you may find yourself somewhere you are not meant to be. It's best to play along and check your ego at the door. Not everything is meant for you, and not everyone is going to want you around. But maybe if you mind your tongue and stay humble, you will be able to find a treasure no one else has ever been privy to behold.

> *Reversed:* It doesn't take much to turn a good situation bad, and right now you may have done the very thing that has flicked the switch. Stomping your

feet in frustration and being ornery will only make things worse. Then again, maybe stirring the pot and causing trouble is exactly what you had hoped to do.

8 of Wands

When the pressure and energy of a volcano get to a certain intensity, it explodes and sends everything around it up and out into the world. As you can see, our mermaid is having trouble catching up to the fire pearl wands that have been launched from the volcanic spout below her. This intense force moves not just the wands but the water as well. It pushes it with an extreme force upward and into the light, below to above. If the mermaid is not careful, she too will be pushed into the world above, ready or not!

> *Upright:* Now is the time. The 8 of Wands has opened a channel to bring all your ideas out of your head and into the physical world. The intensity of this opening is so great that you may feel you are in hyperdrive right now. There is no doubt that you will feel a certain rush and thrill as your ideas are pulled out of the brooding vortex of the mind and thrust into the world of action. Keep in mind that the burst of energy that got you to where you are now headed won't last, nor will it keep you there. Enjoy the ride while you can.

Reversed: If you have not been paying attention to what has been going on in your life, this sudden explosion may cause you more stress and worry than joy and exhilaration. Imagine if the mermaid had not been paying attention, and one of those flying wands hit her in the head on its way to the surface—how painful and dangerous would that have been? You may currently be feeling like you have been hit on the head yourself, now going along kicking and screaming.

9 of Wands

It might look nice and calm in the fire pearl harvesting cave right now, but things can change very quickly. Our fire pearl harvester knows his surroundings well. He has learned over the years not to take the conditions of his workplace for granted. He must be ready and able to deal with any and all unexpected flare-ups or eruptions. Yet if we take a good look at him, he looks meditative as he places the fire pearls atop their awaiting wands. Part of walking the path of awareness is keeping the body and mind calm while being aware of the ever-moving conditions around you.

> *Upright:* Learning to harvest creative energy takes patience and strength. You have to know how to ride the energy when it flows and how to get into the vibration of it when it is calm and quiet. There is a balance that takes place in this card that is not always obvious, but simply knowing it is something you should be aware of will assist you all the same.

> *Reversed:* No doubt there is a darker side to this card, a side that is broody and unhappy with the conditions it now finds itself in. The problem is that creative energy is unpredictable; it is ever-changing

and never rational. You may not like your current conditions but you created them. This is actually good news because now you can also change what you need to change...but only if you can stop brooding and blaming the world for five seconds.

10 of Wands

Deep in the hot, blistering, underwater volcanic caves, a mermaid struggles to bring her last load of wands to the fire pearl harvester. Here the water is filled with smoke and ash, making it difficult to not only see but also breathe. The heaviness of the wands combined with the need to breath deeper than normal taxes the mermaid's body. It takes tremendous strength and stamina for her to complete her tasks day in and day out. Yet complete them she must, for her job will not be complete until she has finished what she started.

> *Upright:* It is hard to tell if our mermaid is feeling the pinch of a long, hard, work week or if she is just having one of those days that seems like it won't end. This is often how it feels when one is coming to the end of a creative project. The heaviness of the project starts to take its toll, and all of a sudden you realize just how depleted you truly are. Yet despite the fact that you feel like you are dragging yourself through the volcanic smoke and ash, you must keep your eye squarely on the finish line.

Reversed: So close yet so far. Here is where a lot of people give in, lay their weary bodies down, and let it all go. Right now you may be second-guessing yourself and wondering how you ever allowed yourself to get into this state to begin with. Just remember that this is not the beginning—things are ending, but how you end this energy is totally up to you. Will it be in failure, or will you suck it up and get the job done?

The Page of Wands

The young Page of Wands is just learning how to use her fire pearl. She knows that it holds great power and magic, which is why she steadies it with one hand while she holds tightly with the other. She does not want to be the one who drops or destroys her very first fire pearl. Instead, she is going to take her time and listen very carefully to those who are teaching her how to harness her wand's gift. This young page wants to master her power, even if she makes a few mistakes or miscalculations along the way. She knows missteps won't be the end of the world; instead, they will serve as the very lessons she needs to learn to refine and focus her fire pearl's energy.

Upright: The Page of Wands is asking you to honor and respect your creative gifts, for it is where your true power lies. Hold these gifts carefully yet with authority. Take your time and understand that failing is all part of the process. This little page says that practice makes perfect, so try and try again.

Reversed: Impatience and ignorance will turn your beginning steps into your final march of shame. You are taking only the first steps with this new energy, and you can't possibly know all there is to learn. If you persist in letting your ego run the show, don't be surprised when your fire pearl blows up your brand new wand.

The Knight of Wands

Sentinel duty is part of being a knight of the court of fire. Court life under the rule of the volcano goddess is full of peril, which is why this knight stands at the ready for whatever may come his way. Good or bad, he is prepared. His training has made him alert, responsive, and ready to act when and where it is necessary. This may seem boring and mundane to some, but they don't understand the benefits of commitment, repetition, and duty. For this knight, honor is serving his court with dignity, courage, and unquestionable loyalty.

> *Upright:* When the Knight of Wands comes dancing into your life, you can rest assured that all your hard work and training are coming to a head. Pretty soon you will get to showcase all the wonderful new skills you have spent hours and hours refining. Your sacrifices will soon be worth it, so be vigilant and remain on the lookout. You will need to be able to identify what an opportunity looks like and what a hazardous distraction looks like as well.

Reversed: It is easy to become complacent, thinking that what you are doing is worthless and no longer worthy of your time. Now imagine what would happen if our knight thought that standing his post was not worth his time and something horrible happened to those who rely on him to stay safe, even if they have lived without incident for hundreds of years. The thing is, you just never know when you are going to need to act. You have no idea when someone or something will cross your path that will warrant your complete and utter focus and concentration. Slacking off and not taking your training and skills seriously may end up harming more than just yourself in the long run.

The Queen of Wands

Pele, goddess of creation and destruction knows the depths of her potential only too well. She knows when and where to use that power to create life and when to end a cycle that no longer serves anyone or anything. She controls the ebb and flow of liquid fire, the blood of the earth. Its veins are her domain. She is not interested in small, petty things; instead, her mind is focused on expansion, growth, and the necessary destruction for newness to get a foothold. Attachment is not something she has time for. In order to keep up with the ever-shifting and changing earth, she has to be ready to act at a moment's notice.

Upright: The Queen of Wands teaches us that life and death are one and the same. Where things grow, others die. Where things expand, others contract. Despite this paradox, she wants you to act, move forward, and create something new, exciting, and unlike anything you have ever done before. She knows that something in your life needs to be pulled down or destroyed so that the new thing can take its place. Take a moment to tune into the fiery power of Pele and let her energy seep into your veins. Let her show you where to wield your creative power and how to create something meaningful, passionate, and full of intent.

Reversed: Do you know what happens when you don't use the fire inside of you? It does one of two things: it burns out or rages out of control. One of these two is happening to you right now. You are either overly reactionary and are finding yourself triggered by everything or everyone, or you are finding it hard to be inspired. When you don't capitalize on the queen's gift, it will turn on itself and become self-destructive. The trick to this card is finding the balance between creative potential and burnout. Only you will know what that balance is for you and your current situation.

The King of Wands

The shark king, Kamohoalii, takes his job as protector and ruler very seriously. The waters and lands of his kingdom are abundant and rich, and many a troublemaker has tried and failed to infiltrate his peaceful and productive kingdom. In order for his queen to fulfill her duties, he must first fulfill his own. With his fire pearl at full power, he patrols the boundaries of his realm, protected by the many sharks at his command. He makes sure his sentinels are in place and that the wards and protection spells of the fire pearls have not been tampered with. The King of Wands knows only too well that the freedoms and rights of his inhabitants are fragile things—if he is not vigilant, they could very easily be taken away.

Upright: The King of Wands reminds us that power comes with great responsibility and that your place at the top is only as firm as your dedication to lead with commitment and honor. He understands that his strength is not just for him alone but for all who fall under his protection and guidance. Being a leader is not easy, and being one with great power is even harder still. However, despite

his serious nature and commitment to the betterment of his realm, he will also act instantly and without hesitation. The King of Wands is a doer, not a dreamer and his boundless energy serves his duties well.

Reversed: It can be easy to forget that predators are dangerous. Hunting, stalking, and killing is part of their nature. This behavior is not something for which they feel guilt or remorse, as it is part of who they are. Remember too that despite the predator's cool calculation, they don't always get their prey. In fact, they often miss more than they hit, which builds a high level of resilience in them. If you are finding that you are missing your target more often than not at the moment, know that a deeper lesson is playing out. Your resilience muscles have weakened and need to be strengthened. So instead of throwing fireballs with all of your might and fury, use this time to strengthen your resolve and get in touch with your inner predator.

THE SUIT OF
Pentacles

Ace of Pentacles

What would you do if you found a trunk full of treasure? Are you prepared for the changes this opportunity will bring with it? From the mermaids' perspective, these shiny trinkets have no real value other than looking pretty. But how do you see the opportunity the ace brings you? All that glitters is not gold no matter how much you want it to be. Opportunities tend to not solve a problem; in fact, they tend to bring even more things to sort out with them. Finding hidden treasure can be fun, but was it really about the find or the journey you took to find it?

Upright: The Ace of Pentacles speaks of a beginning, a possible new adventure. It always lets you know that on the flip side of this coin there is much more work to be done. Finding the treasure is one thing, but knowing what to do next is quite another. Roll up your sleeves, because now that the ace has shown up, the real work begins.

Reversed: Sometimes we can't see a gift even when it is dropped right in our laps. Things are nowhere nearly as bad as you are making them out to be, and you do have the chance to make them even better. That's why it's too bad you can't see how this is the first step to a much more pleasant journey.

2 of Pentacles

Can you juggle as well as this rabbit? Really, how many people do you know who can stand on one leg while riding a fish and balancing two coins? I don't know about you but this rabbit just looks like a bit of a show off. But at least the mer-children look amused. We all need a bit of entertainment in our lives, and this rabbit really knows how to put on a show.

Upright: There is a bit of the dramatic in the 2 of Pentacles like it is all just for show, perhaps. While you may be balancing two things at once, things are really nowhere near as bad as you are making out. Then again, how on earth would you get anyone to take notice of you if you didn't add a bit of drama to your routine?

Reversed: While the rabbit seems to understand that he is merely showing off a new trick, you have started to identify with the act itself. The "look at me" aspect of your theatrics has now taken over your life, and where before it was all just for show, you will find you really do have a problem on your hands if you are not careful.

3 of Pentacles

Have you heard the saying "many hands make light work?" Everyone has special gifts and skills, and when people come together to help each other or collaborate, things get done quickly and harmoniously. The 3 of Pentacles reminds us that our differences are our strengths; we were never all meant to be the same. We can create something beautiful while working together. It could be as simple as a frog queen, a mermaid, and a sprite all coming together to harvest flowers for an upcoming celebration.

Upright: Now is the time to call on the talents of others. You may have skill but it is not enough to pull off what you want to create. You are going to need help from people who think and create differently than you. When you can build a team where everyone gets to play to their strengthens, you will be unstoppable.

Reversed: You can resist help at your own detriment. You may think you can do this on your own but you are wrong. Keep going down this path and you will end up wasting time and money you will never get back.

4 of Pentacles

Do you ever find yourself getting bored with your life? I know the feeling. Sitting here on my rock, all I can bring myself to care about is my hair, stroking it one full brush stroke at a time … sitting, brushing, and thinking of nothing or no one. There is something to be said for allowing ourselves to lean in and get comfortable with boredom. For between each brush stroke, my mind clears and all I have is the moment, this moment, the one where there is nothing but me, the sound of the waterfall and the feel of each brush stroke moving through my hair.

> *Upright:* The 4 of Pentacles has a lot to teach you about getting back in touch with the moment. You may have placed yourself in a state of paralysis or disengagement, but this is not exactly what you need right now. Instead, allow yourself to reconnect with the ordinary, everyday experience of life. When you are connected and grounded in the moment, it is easier to let go and find a new interest in something that was not there before.

Reversed: Have you ever stopped yourself from engaging with the world around you because you thought it might take something from you or cost you too much? This kind of fear isolates you and disconnects you from the simple joys of being alive. You can't stay on the rock forever. You must eventually move, despite your fears.

Notes: _____

_____

_____

_____

_____

_____

_____

_____

_____

_____

_____

_____

_____

_____

_____

_____

_____

_____

_____

_____

_____

_____

_____

_____

_____

5 of Pentacles

What you want is right there, waiting for you to acknowledge it. The mermaid is holding the solution to your current issue, problem, or dilemma ... but you can't see it. The fact is that when your brain is focused on the problem, all it will see is more problems. So even though the mermaid is in plain sight, you just cannot see the assistance being offered to you.

Upright: When we are disconnected or out of alignment with the very thing we say we want, we won't see it, even if it's right in front of us. This card is a warning that your current point of attraction is being guided by the problem, not the solution. Change your mindset and you will see the beautiful mermaid and all she has to offer.

Reverse: You have finally figured out that you are not alone, but you still can't quite make out who else is right there with you. Luckily for you, this mermaid guide is patient and more than willing to help you align to her vibration. Take your time and contine to let the receptive energy reframe your awareness— before you know it, you'll be able to reach out and take the offerings from your mermaid guide.

6 of Pentacles

Oxygen is an important element of water. Without it, nothing can live in the water, especially the mer-folk. At a very young age, mer-children are taught how to oxygenate the water where they live. This not only benefits them but everyone who lives in or near the water itself. It is, in many respects, an act of survival that keeps on giving. With each new oxygen bubble added to the water, the value of the water itself and the land around it increases. What a gift these young children are giving to everyone around them.

> *Upright:* How can you add value to the world around you? It is not very often that people stop and think about how they can add to the world rather than take from it, but that is exactly what you are being asked to consider here in the 6 of Pentacles. Take a lesson from the mer-children and remember that it should be something that is easy yet necessary to not just you but everyone around you.

> *Reversed:* Can you imagine if instead of the mer-children adding oxygen to the water they were taking it out? The results would be disastrous. When we take from a place of fear and greed, we

don't just harm others but we also endanger the very environment we live in. You are being asked to check that fear and lack-filled thinking at the door before you destroy something you can never bring back.

Notes: _____

_____

_____

_____

_____

_____

_____

_____

_____

_____

_____

_____

_____

_____

_____

_____

_____

_____

_____

_____

_____

_____

_____

_____

_____

7 of Pentacles

There is nothing like seeing your goals come together. There is a wonderful sense of accomplishment in knowing you are almost at the finish line. Almost, but not quite. Just like our mer-couple, they are not yet finished with the creation phase known as pregnancy. They know they are getting really close to the birth of their creation but there is still some time to go. Yet despite the waiting, they know the result is all but certain.

Upright: You have worked hard and are finally starting to see results of all those hours working away to achieve your current goals. But you are not there just yet and now would be the worst time ever to take your foot off the gas. Instead dig deep and work harder so you can get yourself across the finish line.

Reversed: Now would be a good time to remember there is your time and then a little something called "divine time." You may not like being on divine time but that is exactly where you now find yourself. You are impatient and trying to push something into being that is not ready. Stop or you will blow up all your good work.

8 of Pentacles

Have you ever wondered how different the world would look if we all knew there was enough to go around and that we would all be taken care of by our community? This is one thing the fae and mer-folk know. Everyone has a gift and plays a special part in their world, and no one will ever go without. Here in the 8 of Pentacles the smallest and tallest line up to offer what they have in order to receive their fair share. This is the lesson of value—when we value who we are, so will those around us. It doesn't matter if you are a toad, faerie or fox, you matter and you are worthy.

Upright: You may very well be seeing signs of your good work starting to manifest around you, but now is not the time to become complacent or get a big head. You have much more work to do; people are now expecting to see more of your work. You have started to create buzz around who you are, and what you do and now is the time to capitalize on it.

Reversed: So people know your name … big deal. If you think you have finally made it, you are sadly mistaken. Sitting back and basking in the half-glow of your work might make our ego feel good, but it will be very temporary because you will have missed the real opportunity this card brings with it. The value of this card is all about how you contribute. Miss this lesson now and you will be doomed to repeat it.

9 of Pentacles

You slowly walk toward the wishing well and toss in your coin. You take a deep breath and release your wish to the rippling water below. You touch your heart and lips and turn around. Without looking back, you walk away. Just then, the keeper of the well raises and adds your coin to her collection. Your wish may or may not be answered, yet the mermaid of the well continues to collect your coins and add them to her collection. She receives without asking and gets to be the keeper of the wants and wishes of others. When you look at all of her coins can you find yours?

> *Upright:* There is a protective element to the 9 of Pentacles like you have finally learned how to set boundaries around yourself, your health, and your material treasures. Just as the mermaid keeps the coins and secrets of the well protected, there is nothing wrong with protecting what you have worked so hard to create, especially if you intend to keep enjoying your good fortune for a long time to come.

Reversed: It is important to remember that not everyone is a threat and not everyone wants what you have. Here in the reversed aspect of the 9 of Pentacles, there can be a tendency to become paranoid about losing all that you have created. All this line of thinking will do is suck the joy out of the life you have worked so hard to build. Didn't you create what you did to enjoy it, not to imprison yourself?

10 of Pentacles

There is a saying that goes something like "the more you bless, the more blessings you have." Here at the mermaid feast they are not only counting their blessings but they are sharing them. Sharing one's blessing is the greatest way to honor them. This family of mermaids knows it is blessed and also understand that the more they honor those blessings, the more blessing they will have to share with those around them.

Upright: The 10 of Pentacles reminds us that we often have more then we think we do. By taking a mental inventory of all that we have, we come to see we are in a much better place than our fears and doubts want us to believe. Just for today, bless your blessings and then see how you can share them with those close to you and in your local community

Reversed: Despite having everything you need and require, you are still holding tight to your vibration of lack. What is the point of having all you need if you are so scared to even use it to better your life? Now might be a very good time to ask yourself: when will enough be enough?

The Page of Pentacles

Do you remember how you used shiny things to bounce light when you were a child? You used glass, silver trays, mirrors—anything that would send the sunlight back onto something else and create a sunspot or rainbow. I remember my own children discovering this trick in much the same way as the young page. Realizing they could make rainbows on purpose was a true joy to my children. To see that they could use one thing and deliberately create a desired result would leave them with huge smiles on their faces. In this card, the young page also looks pretty happy with himself, as he has just realized that given the right set of conditions, he can create something at will.

> *Upright:* Creation is meant to be fun. You are meant to play and explore and see how things work together. Here with the Page of Pentacles, you are getting permission to simply play, to use what's around you and see what might result. Just like the page in the card you may find you will be happily surprised to find that you can create something you want on purpose.

Reversed: All children have the potential to be pouty, bored, and lacking in motivation to play. Right now, you don't see the point in doing anything just for the fun of it. Nothing seems to pique your interest enough to get you off the couch. It's not that you are afraid you won't be able to create what you want but that you think you are somehow beyond this stage. You're not. Don't allow your mistaken sense of progression let you miss the perfect conditions that now provide you with the means to learn something new and create something you never thought possible.

The Knight of Pentacles

The young knight stops under the shade of an ancient tree by the sacred lake, in the kingdom of Pentacles to take notes from her morning's patrol. She has found that walking the boundaries of her required area suit her better. She can take her time and make sure she doesn't miss anything. Things on the ground are much easier to miss when you are astride a horse. Slowly and methodically she does her rounds, marking her findings one by one in her leather-bound ledger. Details are important to this knight. Battles can be won and lost in the margins, and this knight is more than equipped to win. With quill in hand and pentacle strapped to her side, she prefers the steady, consistent hard work her post offers. She is more than happy to leave the shouting and fanfare to other knights of the realm.

Upright: There is no pomp and ceremony attached to your current situation, but don't let that stop you from giving it your all. Now is a time for quiet observation, as you will soon need to take slow, methodical, and deliberate movements. Speed is your enemy at the moment, so stop trying to rush through this current step or problem. There is something you need to be aware or take note of,

and you can't do it properly if you are only focused on the end result. Be like the knight: stop, take stock of the moment, and record what you see, hear, and feel. It will be of benefit later.

Reversed: No matter how much you want to run full speed ahead or leave where you currently are, you will find yourself blocked and slowed at every turn. Resisting this enforced slower pace will only mean having to stay in this spot longer than is needed. The choice is yours: surrender and let this pass at its own pace, or keep fighting and stay stuck.

The Queen of Pentacles

The Lady of the Lake is one water deity you do not want to mess with. Forged in the deepest legends, she seems to have found a place amongst the misty vales of Avalon. Her waters are healing and transformative. Many have come to her lake to restore themselves, or in some cases, to be reborn. She, herself, is known as the creator of leaders, warriors, and kings. It is from her water that all things physical are born. As she holds her pentacle high above her head, she commands the energy of the water, the power of the air, and the strength of the earth to come together and benefit all within her kingdom. There is nothing in her realm that she does not know, heal, or manifest.

Upright: The Queen of Pentacles is a grounded, healing force. Self-care is a full-time lifestyle, not just an every-so-often luxury, which is why her lake is so healing. You can dangle your feet in her lake and feel all the tension seep out of your toes and away from your body. As you sit there allowing her to heal and restore you, she is probing your heart's desire. She is seeing what gift she can give you to help you become the best version of yourself. She is in tune with your karmic path and has a real talent for picking visionaries and innovators. If she has revealed herself to you, she thinks you are worth more than you are currently investing in yourself.

Reversed: When the Queen of Pentacles is having some downtime, she does it the same way she does everything—completely and totally. She shuts it all down. If you feel like maybe you have been disconnected from her healing energy and shut out from her manifestation circle, that's because you have. Now is not the time to come to the queen with your list of demands. Instead, honor her and give her time to replenish and restore.

The King of Pentacles

In order to understand the material world, one must first learn about flow. In order to truly understand and master flow, one must be tethered to the energy of the physical world. In other words, to become the King of Pentacles means being grounded yet flowing, much like Conduits, god of rivers. Rivers sculpt, cut, and reshape the physical world. They literally slice their way through hard and solid places to create a flowing, living, stream of abundance. Where there was once a barren landscape, a river brings life. In order to keep life evolving and growing, healthy and strong, the waters of the river need to be clean, clear and always moving. It is this paradox of stability and flow, that the King of Pentacles has mastered. He knows that in order to be grounded and secure, one must enter the flowing river of manifestation. In order to have ongoing health, well-being and prosperity, one must be able to maintain steady footing while allowing the body to consistently move. Holding without holding on is the lesson we must learn while in Conduits's presence.

Upright: There is an unwavering confidence in the King of Pentacles, for he knows he will always have what he needs. He is confident that whatever he requires will show up at the right time and in

the right way, exactly when it is needed. He has worked hard to get where he is today and is more than willing to show you some of his tricks. Just know that the King of Pentacles is the master of the long game. He isn't interested in overnight success or your need for instant gratification. He wants you to build an ever-growing and sustainable life, not just a moment that will be quickly forgotten.

Reversed: It is important to understand that the king is not obligated to share anything with you. As one of his many subjects in his ever-growing kingdom, you will benefit from his mastery on a very basic level, but he owes you nothing beyond that. So if you ask him for something, you must allow him to do so on his terms and in his way if you truly want him to bless you with knowledge and understanding of the material world. Neediness and impatience will only drive this king away, as he wants you to learn that flowing abundance in all of its forms is not a trick but a never-ending process.

THE SUIT OF
Swords

Ace of Swords

Resting deep on the ocean floor, once on the deck of the ship that was transporting it from far away worlds, lays the magical sword of knowledge. A snaking rope moves slowly and heavily with the motion of the waves, keeping the sword in place. All that knowledge and power is simply out in the open waiting for someone to come and claim it. The irony is that this deep down in the ocean, no one cares. What good is this sword to the creatures of the sea? This relic teaches us that the value of all gifts is in the eye of the beholder. This sword might be the very thing you require, but then again maybe its secrets don't interest you at all. Only you will know.

> *Upright:* The Ace of Swords brings with it a gift, secret, or knowing that was unavailable to you before, as you were not in alignment with it. But now that you are and you can see the sword, will you pick it up? Is the offer even relevant anymore? Perhaps the sword offers only the gift of hindsight and we all know how helpful that is. I guess you won't know until you hold it in your hands.

Reversed: Is it really bad to walk away from information you never asked for? In our age of information overload, the Ace of Swords in the reversed position may very well be suggesting an information diet. Hidden deep under the sea, no one can hear the stories the sword of knowledge has to tell and *maybe* that is a good thing. We live in a world of noise already—would you even notice another addition to the orchestra? Remove yourself from all new information for a while and give yourself time to distinguish what is essential and useful for your ears … and what is just noise pollution.

2 of Swords

Sparring is not only a good way to brush up on your technique, but it is also a pretty good workout. There is a level of skill, order, and regimentation regarding sparring. Our strapping mer-man is helping his landlocked friend move his body while also moving his mind. By teaching the mer-man about swordsmanship, he is also allowing a new perspective to enter his reality. What may seem natural and necessary to the human male is strange and dangerous to the mer-man. Yet despite their differences, they both see the benefits sparring creates.

> *Upright:* There are two sides to your current dilemma, each one wanting time and space to argue its case. The question is: Can you release your need to be right and open a non-judgmental space for these two ideas, thoughts, and options to plead their case? Take a lesson from our friends in this card, sparring can be useful. It can move energy, strengthen muscles you never knew you had and build strength and confidence. All very good qualities to have when making a decision.

Reversed: The thing about sparring is that no one really wins and no one really loses, but someone has more skill, force, and will than the other. This truth reflects what is happening inside your head right now: you are refusing to see that one of your options is clearly more capable than the other. For whatever reason, you want both to be feasible but they just are not. Eventually, the idea or option that has the most strength, stamina, and expertise will wear you down. The fight was over before it even begun, you just haven't realized it yet.

3 of Swords

The last shallow breath of a giant of the sea is slowly exhaled, and with it goes the light that carries the whale's soul back to the heavens. The mer-folk weep and grieve as they sit powerlessly while their brethren dies, knowing they are too late to make a difference. The best they can do at this point is be a witness to the whale's passing, giving thanks for its life and ensuring its energy passes from the physical back to the vibrational world. Sometimes this is the part we must play—holding space, respecting the cycles, and honoring the life that has now been extinguished. Painful as it might be to hold that space, it is a sacred act…one that these mer-folk know only too well.

Upright: The 3 of Swords brings pain. Sometimes the pain is yours and sometimes it is not. Either way, you will feel it. There is no getting around the mental anguish your current situation brings, so practice holding the space for it instead. See it as a sacred passing, something that must happen in order for newness to appear. Within pain are the seeds of joy, and one cannot exist without the other, though they are not exactly two equal sides of the same coin. You will find the spiritual lesson in this, but maybe not right this second.

Reversed: The time for grieving is over. You have played your part in the letting go process and now must get back to life. Holding space is a temporary thing, never meant to last longer than the time it takes for energy to pass from one cycle to another. This is your sign to move on. Pick up your three swords and leave this phase behind.

4 of Swords

When you look at this card, can you tell if the young maiden is asleep, dead, or under some sort of preservation spell? You really can't tell at a glance, and that is one of the tricks of this card. How you find respite from your daily grind may not look the same as it does to someone else. How you relax your mind and rejuvenate your body may be very different from how those around you do it. That doesn't make your method—or theirs—wrong.

Upright: The 4 of Swords wants you to take a time-out…a real one, not a half-day-still-checking-emails-kinda break. So what does that look like for you? Will it mean finding somewhere quiet and peaceful to nap? Or will it mean taking yourself to the beach so you can meditate with the waves? Just know that taking this time-out now will only assist you moving forward. It is the reboot your brain needs. If this card has shown up in your reading you are being asked to step back and take a break. You need to remove yourself from your daily life just enough so that you can feel the cobwebs leave your mind. Step away and unwind, the world won't end! Go and relax.

Reversed: You are about to spin into overwhelm. When this card lands upside down, it means you have missed your time-out and now you are paying the price. Worry, stress, and procrastination will be the results that will await you if you do not turn things around.

5 of Swords

"It's all fun and games until someone gets hurt", my mother used to say. It would appear that this saying is exactly the case here in the 5 of Swords. These innocent mer-children have stumbled across human weapons and in their excitement to play with these newfound objects, someone indeed has gotten hurt. The problem with sharp pointy things is that they have the capacity to cause pain and despair. As the young mer-child looks at his flowing blood in horror, his guardian penguin pats him gently on the head, for the penguin is all too aware of the pain and anguish human objects can cause for those who live in the watery world. The other mer-children appear to have stopped in mid-play, unaware of what to do. Their first instinct is to stop the blood flow, for blood in the water will bring even more trouble and possible danger.

> *Upright:* The 5 of Swords is a reminder that everything comes with a price. Sometimes that price is pain, and sometimes it is a good idea gone horribly wrong. The trick to this card is your response to the price. Just like the mer-children, how you respond to the cuts and bruises this card brings with it will determine whether or not the price you have paid for what you want has been worth it.

Reversed: Can you tell by looking at this card who caused the mer-child to bleed? Was it self-inflicted or did one of the other children make the now gushing wound? I doubt that you can tell just by looking at the scene, which is one of the tricky aspects of this card: who's to blame when it all goes wrong? Yet here in the reversed aspect you understand that everything that happens to you at some level is 100 percent your responsibility. To move on and get on with things, you must accept the part you have played. Perhaps you took one for the team, or maybe you just stepped in to make sure things didn't get completely out of hand. Either way, it was your decision and yours alone. Allow that fact to liberate you and move forward.

6 of Swords

The ride across the snow is not exactly a smooth one. Let's face it—seals aren't the most graceful on land. The fact that the mer-tinker has gotten his handmade sleigh to work at all is a victory that might not seem big (it might even look clumsy to an observer), but the tinker will take it all the same. The need to get his sleigh idea working on some level is more important than what the end result looks like. Even though it may be far from perfect, this sleigh could very well save a mermaid's life in the future.

Upright: Sometimes you have to go for the small win. Sometimes it is better to get up and get moving than to wait around for all of the elements to be perfect. You'll have room for navigation later so for now, allow yourself to enjoy your not-so-perfect seal ride across the ice.

Reversed: There is a good chance you are beating yourself up when you should be doing the happy dance. Instead of thinking about how bumpy or uncertain your journey will be, try focusing on the fact that you are no longer stuck or stranded. Life

needs to move, and energy needs to flow, even if it is on the back of a tinker made sleigh bounding across the snow. The way is clear, the vehicle has arrived, and staying put is not an option.

7 of Swords

Human items have found their way onto the ice. With no one around to claim them, the mer-men pick over the items deciding on what they might find useful. This is the way of lost and found things. The person who finds them often makes a decision about ownership. Is this a moral issue or is it a case of finders-keepers? The mer-men find many lost items in the water and on the shoreline. They decide if what they find will serve them. If it benefits many, they take what they need. If it does not, they leave it behind.

> *Upright:* Ideas, thoughts, and beliefs aren't often something we think about owning. Yet we spend an awful amount of energy building our lives around the ideas and beliefs of others. The 7 of Swords asks you to think about what ideas, thoughts, and beliefs serve you. Which ones add to your life and the lives of those around you? Which ones should you give back? Not everything is ours and not everything should be kept. Take what you need and leave the rest for someone who will benefit from it.

Reversed: In life and in art, ideas and concepts are inevitably recycled or repurposed. In many respects, this is the natural evolution of an idea or thought process. You may not be seeing it that way right now, though. Instead, you may be feeling ripped off and used. You may feel that someone else is taking credit for something you believe is rightfully yours. This wounded ego energy may very well be blocking you from seeing things, even if what has been recycled or repurposed still serves you. Maybe it was time to pass it along. Perhaps the thing's time with you has come to a natural end, and like all things has found a new owner. In the same way, the seven swords have now found their way into the hands of the mer-men.

8 of Swords

Is there anything more vulnerable than a mermaid out of water? Exposed to not only the elements but also wild animals and possibly humans, our mermaid is tied up and seemingly helpless. Yet looks can be deceiving, and one never knows what's hidden just beyond the frames of the scene. Our mermaid's spirit animal, the arctic mink may be a clue. The mink loves complexity and thrives on solving problems by pulling information from multiple sources. It seeks a deeper knowing and wants to enjoy all the richness of life. But this means you must be more than the limitations of your circumstances. Our mermaid does appear limited by her circumstances, but in order for her to expand and grow, perhaps this is the point.

> *Upright:* It is time to stop your excuses and move beyond your perceived limitations. Growth means digging deeper, finding new ways to solve current problems, and knowing when to be still, seemingly taking no action at all. What seems like a weakness is actually your biggest asset in this particular circumstance. Use it to your advantage and advance.

Reversed: Let's face it, you are in no hurry to figure any of this out. In fact, you figure that if you tie yourself up for long enough, someone else will do it for you. There is an element of being unavailable in the upside down 8 of Swords, too busy, too confused, too stressed, too out of touch. We both know this is just a ruse, however—you know exactly what you are doing. The catch, however, is that this behavior could very well backfire and the bonds tighten to the point where even you will struggle to break them loose. Games have consequences, and this one has you exposed.

9 of Swords

The horrifying nightly screech of the sirens' song echoes across the water and up to the land above, making it more than impossible for the researcher to sleep. Pushing her hands to her ears to block out the noise, she pinches the side of her glasses to her face. As she peers over the cliff, she wonders how many more nights will she have to endure this torture. Her only solace is that the siren cannot climb the rocky wall of the cliff face. As the night wears on, the sirens' song gets louder and louder, ceasing only with the light of the rising sun. The researcher knows this cannot be sustained; choices will have to be made.

> *Upright:* Conditions right now are less than desirable. You could even say they are keeping you up at night. Everyone and everything are demanding space inside your head, and it is becoming overwhelming. Exhaustion and despair are often the symptoms of overwhelm and stress. Perhaps like our researcher, you need to make some other choices about who and what can pitch a tent inside your head. Set some clear boundaries, and decide to take it one day at a time.

Reversed: It is very easy to look at the scene playing out in this card and think that the person in the tent is the victim. They're just trying to get some sleep, right? But let's consider the fact that this is actually the siren's home. This is where she lives (and screams). The cliff is her lounge, and she is there to do what she always does. She cannot be blamed if someone comes into her home and doesn't like the noise. When you show up in someone else's space, don't expect them to alter it just because you don't like it. Remember that you are the guest—you are the one who is going to have to alter their mindset.

10 of Swords

There is no life that is left behind. Only the empty organic matter that once housed it and the history that will be told of the life that once lived. This is how stories are created, through what is left behind. It is not about crying for what has been lost but instead a celebration of what was left after the fall, the pieces that can be retold. We are left with pieces that come together, merging something that *was* with something that *could be*. Where there is an ending there is also a beginning.

> *Upright:* When it's over, it's over. There are some things in life that we never truly recover from or can never go back and change. They are done, final, and in many respects set in the stone of history's wheel. There is no way the merman who now finds himself face down in the snow is ever getting back up. The life he knew is over. The incarnation he was experiencing is done. He is now someone else's history. This is the way the world of living things is meant to be. It is part of its order. If things don't end and we do not pass into collective history, there will be no place for anything new. What was will never be again and that is a wonderful divine thing.

Reversed: Denial is not healthy. It is not even rational. Everything ends. Everything ceases to have a purpose or use. This is just the way of things. You can beg and plead. You can stomp your feet and shout as loud as you can. You can even get into the "but why?" mantra. None of it will change the fact that something that once was is no more. Doors are closing, something is ending, and the cycle has come to completion. Fight it with all your might if you want, but it won't change the outcome.

The Page of Swords

In the light of the sun deep under the ice shelf, a young page sits and studies the sharp pointy thing she found this morning during her daily lessons. It was just sitting in the snow, all alone without nothing and no one around it, as if waiting for her to come and discover it. Now that she has it though, she has no idea what to do with it. In fact, this young page doesn't even know what it is or what it is used for, let alone that it is a dangerous weapon. All she knows is that if she holds it just right, it sparkles in the filtered sunlight. She doesn't understand the pain this object could cause if the user is not taught to wield it correctly. Then again, that is why she is a page. Everything is a lesson to learn and a mystery to solve.

> *Upright:* When they first appear, thoughts and ideas can seem harmless. They tickle our imagination, filling our heads with images and our bodies with emotions. Initially, they feel exciting and new. However, not all thoughts should be held onto, and not all ideas should be brought into the physical world. This is where the lesson of decrement comes in, the knowledge of what is life-affirming and what will bring us pain. Like the page, you are just starting in your lessons, the lines still seem

blurred. But given enough time and enough practice, you will learn to wield your own sword, the sword of discernment.

Reversed: Like the lessons of all the pages, you may think this one does not apply to you. You consider yourself already well-groomed in making decisions and don't understand why you should have to go back to basics and retrain your mind. The truth is, you are not as good as you think at deciding which thoughts are helpful, which habits are supportive, and which flashes of inspiration to follow. You have made numerous mistakes and have not seen any substantial results, so the page has swum into your life to offer assistance. Take a step back, and see where you could be more active and less impulsive in your decision making, just for a moment. It surely can't hurt.

The Knight of Swords

Ideas come and ideas go. The ones that stick around do so for a reason. These ideas are ready to make a commitment and are asking you to do the same. They want you to play your part and honor your role in the co-creation process. Our young knight understands this level of commitment, for every day she must show up and train. Following through, showing up even when you don't want to, and understanding that sometimes what you co-create has little or nothing to do with you personally is true committment. The knight of swords purpose is to serve her kingdom to the best of her ability. This is why she must continue to focus, clear her mind of distractions, and commit to her process.

> *Upright:* If the Knight of Swords has shown up in your reading, you are being asked to commit to an idea. This is not just any idea but one that will move you closer to your purpose or life's dream. You must be willing to give this idea your full and clear mind and be willing to work with it each and every day. As only this level of commitment will earn you the results you require.

Reversed: You and your idea are out of alignment. Stop trying to control the terms and conditions of your mind and instead clear it and open up to the possibility that awaits you. Ride the energy of the wave like the knight, don't try to control it or you shall sink.

The Queen of Swords

Do you know the story of the Snow Queen? I don't mean the one written by men, but the real story … her story. She is a winter goddess who has real power, compassion, and intellectual prowess. The Snow Queen rules the season of winter. She is interested in all things cold and frozen. It is up to her to make sure that the world has a balance of silent, still restoration and busy, sun-filled days. She cares for all those who live in the extremes of the poles, tending to their needs and keeping the peace between all who reside there. Her kingdom is vast and her responsibilities immense, yet you will never hear her complain. This is who she is; this is her true form—the keeper of reason, order, and harsh realities.

Upright: The Snow Queen governs some of the most extreme territories in the world. Conditions are very rarely favorable, yet she must get on with her job. Regardless of her harsh environment, others still look to her for guidance and leadership. She needs to keep her mind focused and decisions swift. You may find you are walking in the footsteps of the Snow queen right now. Your situation may not be ideal and it may seem like everything is against you but you have to keep going. Others are depending on you to stay the course and lead the way.

Reversed: We don't always want to be the one that has to solve everyone else's problems. Sometimes we just wish the outside world would go away and leave us the hell alone. With the Snow Queen upside down, you may find you are blasting people with your cold-heartedness more than you mean to. You may require a break or time for quiet self-reflection, but don't forget that you will have to eventually reap the frozen, harsh energy you now sow.

The King of Swords

When the cold winds of winter whip through your clothes and pull at your hair, you know that Boreas, the god of the north wind is awake. From his throne in the winter palace, he commands the blustery breezes of the winter season, sending chilly air through the mountain passes and into city streets. He commands the direction and intensity of the winds as well as the storms of the coldest months of the year. During this time he must be alert and on guard, never wavering at his post.

Upright: The King of Swords has gained a position of mastery. He has earned his title through hard work and discipline. He bears the full brunt of the responsibilities that land on his shoulders. He alone must do what is required in the time it will take. The king teaches us what it means to be committed to our ideas and beliefs. He shows us how to master our minds and fulfill our tasks through action. Never underestimate the importance of your role and the ideals you live by.

Reversed: All kings have a rebellious nature. They all want to leave their mark on the world and be seen as special and unique. Often this line of thinking

becomes corrupted by the king's ego, and chaos ensues. If you have become more interested in being a rebel without a clue, then clueless is exactly how you will be remembered. People will not look back on your work or life as something noble but instead as something disruptive and annoying. It might seem easier to use that big sword to get your way, but that is not really what makes a leader. You can lead or rebel, but you can't do both.

Chapter 5

MERMAID MAGIC AND SPREADS

What could be better than a little mermaid magic? Many consider mermaids magical creatures who have the ability to change the direction of the wind, make waves, and even cause lightning. All of these magical properties move magical energy either towards you or away from you, depending on how attuned you are into the mermaids' magical gifts. The following simple spells will assist you to tune in and tap into the magical energy the mermaids can bring to your daily life. These spells cover the "big three": health, love, and money. No matter what is going on in your life, one of these three will draw you to the mermaids' magic, so let the winds of fortune, the waves of healing, or the lightning bolts of love find you.

A SPELL FOR HEALING

"Healing" is a very broad term, but you will know if there are areas in your life that require healing energy. Perhaps you have experienced a disagreement with someone you care about and wish to heal the current rift or tension. Maybe you have a past wound that needs to be dealt with once and for all. Or perhaps you have a physical issue that needs to recover and mend. All these things will benefit from this spell.

You will need the following cards from your deck:

- 4 of Swords

- Temperance

- Ace of Cups

You will also need:

- A candle

- Crystals (any you feel drawn to add)

Find a quiet, peaceful place to lay your cards, the candle, and the crystals. Make sure this place will not be disturbed for a full 24 hours. If you already have a small altar for spell and ritual work, place your cards there.

Once you have your cards and other magical items laid out, close your eyes and take a couple of nice, deep breaths. Center yourself.

Light your candle and focus on the flame as you continue to breathe slowly and deeply.

Once you feel settled, focused, and fully present, repeat the spell that follows.

When you have completed the verse, I recommend leaving the candle to burn out. If that is not possible, blow the candle out but do not touch anything on the altar for 24 hours.

Note that it really doesn't matter what order you place the cards in or what items you do or do not have to accompany them. All that matters is that you are fully present and aware as you recite the spell itself.

Temperance, please hear my call
For on my knees I now fall
The Sirens' song, send to me
And let the healing energy be
Overflowing like the Ace of Cups
I let it come, I will not block
Instead I shall lie in wait
With the 4 of Swords as my healing mate
Temperance, mix and spin your cups
And from the ace I shall sup
Drinking in your elixir divine
Restore my body and calm my mind
With the mermaids' aid I shall find
Well-being, health, and rifts repaired
With wind and fire and water all
I release this spell,
I cast forth this call!

A SPELL FOR LOVE

This spell is not just for lovers or those wishing to draw a new mate to them—it can also be used for self-love or as part of a self-care ritual. This spell is more about your heart's desire than anything else. Let's face it, heart-centered love is the deepest, the most romantic, and so very whole. All mermaids know that what is in their hearts will always outdo whatever is in their heads.

You will need the following cards from your deck:

- The Star
- 2 of Cups
- 4 of Wands

You will also need:

- A candle
- Crystals (any you feel drawn to add)

Find a quiet, peaceful place to lay your cards and the candle and crystals. Make sure this place will not be disturbed for a full 24 hours. If you already have a small altar for spell and ritual work, place your cards there.

Once you have your cards and other magical items laid out, go ahead and close your eyes. Take a couple of nice deep breaths and center yourself.

Light your candle and focus on the flame as you continue to breathe slowly and deeply.

Once you feel settled, focused, and fully present, place your hand over your heart and repeat the spell that follows.

When you have completed the verse, I recommend leaving the candle to burn out. If that is not possible, blow the candle out and do not touch anything on the altar for 24 hours.

Note that it really doesn't matter what order you place the cards in or what items you do or do not have to accompany them. All that matters is that you are fully present and aware as you recite the spell itself.

Under the sparkling starlight
Beside the flowing river bed
I steady my heart and ready my head
For here in the glow of the Star's bright light
I send this spell and raise my plight
Bring to me my heart's desire
The love I know I require
Steadfast like the 4 of Wands
I sing to you, Star, this lover's song
Although my heart be whole and true
Something new is now overdue
A new experience
A new thrill
Something to excite me
Something flowing yet still
I am not looking to be fulfilled
Nor am I broken and in need of fixing
Rather I rejoice under the stable energy of the 4 of Wands
Resolute, ready, and merry
Strong and bright just like you, Star
Fill my second cup to the brim
With your loving light supply
The love that now awaits mine side.
A hand to hold
A heart to hear
A fresh approach
A new adventure

A new love true and bold
I am ready, hear my call
As it is spoken so it is done.

A SPELL FOR MONEY

Money isn't just something you put in your purse, wallet, pocket, or bank accounts. It is one of many forms of currency. Any resource that brings a better quality of life is a form of currency and currency is what money is. So don't be surprised if money is not the only thing that shows up after you have completed this spell. It very well could be a promotion, the offer of a friend's holiday cabin for free, or even an unexpected gift of the very thing you have been dreaming about.

You will need the following cards from your deck:

- The Knight of Wands
- 9 of Pentacles
- The Sun

You will also need:

- A candle
- Crystals (any you feel drawn to add)

Find a quiet, peaceful place to lay your cards and a candle and any crystals you feel drawn to add. Make sure this place will not be disturbed for a full 24 hours. If you already have a small altar for spell and ritual work, place your cards there.

Once you have your cards and other magical items laid out, close your eyes, take a couple of nice deep breaths, and center yourself.

Light your candle and focus on the flame as you continue to breathe slowly and deeply. Think of the candle as a representation of the Sun card's energy. As you gaze at the flickering flame, feel the Sun amplifying and expanding the circle of light around you.

Once you feel settled, focused and fully present, repeat the spell below

When you have completed the verse, I recommend leaving the candle to burn out. If that is not possible, blow the candle out but do not touch anything on the altar for 24 hours.

Note that the order the cards are placed in or whatever items you do or do not have to accompany them doesn't really matter. All that matters is that you are fully present and aware as you recite the spell itself.

In the garden I shall be
The 9 of Pentacles surrounding me
The Sun's warm glow does heat my skin
And abundance grows deep within
That which lies in my heart's desire
Speaks to the universe like a fire
Alighting the wand the knight does carry
To bring me my wants and marry my needs
The knight rides on with great speed
I stay awaiting here in this place
Counting the disks which take up space
All that I need is drawn to me now
Spreading like wildfire throughout this hour
The blessing they shall align as if pulled to me
For the nine and the knight will make it be
And under the rays of the suns light
I shall sit and await this future made bright
And so it is and so it shall be

DAILY JOURNAL PROMPT SPREAD

Although single-card readings are still technically spreads, it may be better to think of this as a daily mermaid prompt. The daily one-card draw is a really good way to connect to your deck and get a feel for your new cards. This type of spread allows you to build a closer relationship with the deck's individual cards. Personally, I am a daily draw devotee. The simple single-card prompt is sometimes the quickest and most efficient way to get needed information in the moment you need it.

The daily journal prompt is very easy: all you need to do is pick up your deck, shuffle cards while you take a couple of deep, cleansing, breaths, ask the mermaids for your daily message, and select a card. You're selecting one card, and *only* one card. No matter how tempting it may be to draw another, take just the one. Once you have your single card face up and in front of you, follow the steps as mapped out in chapter 2.

I recommend doing the single-card prompt first thing in the morning so you can see how this card shows up or guides you throughout the day. At the end of the day, you can do the following journal prompts as a point of reflection on the card's morning message and how the story played out during your daily activities, if at all.

Journal prompts:

- How did this card show up today?

- How did the card's message resonate with me?

- What elements of this card stood out during my daily routine?

- How is this card and its message a blessing?

- What obstacles or challenges did this card bring in to my day?

TWO HEADS ARE BETTER THAN ONE SPREAD

One of the things I love about the tarot is that each card can change, morph, bend, and flex depending on the other cards around it. Much the way each of us tends to be different around other people in certain social or work situations, the cards themselves are not fixed in the manner in which they show up. In fact, their flexibility is why I like playing around as much as possible with this spread. This spread (or double-card draw, if you like) also helps you build a deeper relationship to your cards. It will help you understand how they speak, interact, and morph to suit the company they find themselves in.

You can use this spread as a quick way to answer a question or simply add it to your tarot journal. One of the upsides to this spread is that you don't even have to ask a question. You could randomly pick two cards out of your deck and read them together. You could also shuffle your deck until two cards fall out, pair them up, and read them together. What about choosing one card and continually changing the cards you pair it with? You would be surprised how differently the Hermit looks when paired with one of the more social cards like the 3 of Cups, the 6 of Pentacles, or the 4 of Wands.

So what are you waiting for? Get your cards and experience how two heads are better than one!

WHAT, WHERE, HOW THREE-CARD SPREAD

Most questions can be answered by a trusty three-card spread. In many ways, they can be adapted to just about anything you need. This simple spread is one of my go-to spreads. It is a great spread to use when you have been suffering from procrastination or if you truly don't know what your next step or action should be. The beauty about this simple spread is that you don't even need to focus on anything in particular. In this spread, the cards do all the work for you.

This spread asks three very simple questions:

Card 1: What one thing needs your attention now?

Card 2: Where is your focus best spent in regards to this one thing?

Card 3: How does this one thing help you with your current problem or situation?

Lay your cards out either in a row or in a column. The formation is not important, as long as you remember what card is first and what card is third. Take your time and enjoy your three-card spread.

THE FOUR ELEMENTS SPREAD

For this spread you are going to have to separate your deck out into five piles. First, suits should be in their own piles from ace through tens, pages, knights, queens, and kings. Then sort out the major arcana cards into the other, Fool through World. That means you will have a pile for wands, a pile for cups, a pile for swords, a pile for pentacles, and a pile with your major arcana cards (the ones with Roman numerals on them). Make sure all piles are face down.

Although mermaids live in the water, they are very skilled at adapting all the elements to be useful, and in this spread they want to show you how to use the elements for guidance and assistance. Pick up the pile of major arcana cards and shuffle them, keeping them face down. Think about your question. Bring it into your mind's eye like a fully formed sentence. Keeping it face down, select one card and place it on the table or reading cloth in front of you. Pick up the pile of swords cards and again shuffle them while keeping your mind on your question. Again draw one card and place it directly above the first card you drew, keeping it face down. Now pick up your cups pile and do the same thing, but place this card to the right of the first card. Now pick up your pentacles pile, hold your focus on your question, draw your card and place it directly under your first card. Now pick up your last pile of cards, the wands, and draw your card, placing it to the left of your first card. What you should have is your major arcana card surrounded by the four elements: air above, earth below, water to the right, and fire to the left.

> *Card 1 Major Arcana*—Each major arcana card is a step along a cyclic path, from the beginning of the fool to the completion energy of the world. Where do you now find yourself along the path of your current situation or problem?

> *Card 2 Swords*—How are the winds of change blowing? Do they favor you or do they offer you resistance?

> *Card 3 Cups*—What is the flow of this situation or problem? Is the water flowing where it needs to or is it moody and stagnate?

> *Card 4 Pentacles*—How solid and strong is your commitment to getting the result you desire?

> *Card 5 Wands*—Fire can burn with resolve or burn with anger, how is your fire burning and is it burning in your favor or is it cutting a path to destruction?

Take your time with this spread, don't rush it. Sit with the cards and really engage with the oracles of the elements.

A Final Note

Congratulations, you have made it to the final lap of the Mermaid Tarot. By now you have had a chance to take a swim with your cards, tried your hand at the spells and taken a deep dive with the four spreads provided in this guide book. You will have made friends with some of the characters on the cards and perhaps even connected with one or more of the gods and goddesses of the mer-folk court. Hopefully you have enjoyed your time here in the waters of the Mermaid Tarot and want to keep the energy of this deck flowing and moving even when the cards are not in your hands. In many ways, holding the cards is just the beginning of your ongoing relationship with the energy this deck emanates. Some of the ways you can carry the energy of the mer-folk with you is through pathwork, ritual, and daily mantras. I also suggest picking up more books on tarot, mermaids, sea magic, and moonology. Another way is to join our community on Instagram—just use the hashtag #MermaidTarotLR in your posts.

The mermaids and I have very much enjoyed our time with you, and we thank you for spending time with us. May your journey be a happy and prosperous one.

Until next time,

Leeza

Notes: _____

_____

_____

_____

_____

_____

_____

_____

_____

_____

_____

_____

_____

_____

_____

_____

_____

_____

_____

_____

_____

_____

_____

_____

Notes: _____
_____
_____
_____
_____
_____
_____
_____
_____
_____
_____
_____
_____
_____
_____
_____
_____
_____
_____
_____
_____
_____

Notes: _____

_____

_____

_____

_____

_____

_____

_____

_____

_____

_____

_____

_____

_____

_____

_____

_____

_____

_____

_____

_____

_____

_____

_____

Notes: _____

_____

_____

_____

_____

_____

_____

_____

_____

_____

_____

_____

_____

_____

_____

_____

_____

_____

_____

_____

_____

_____

_____